Beyond the Reading Wars

edited by
Robyn Ewing

PETA

First published June 2006
by the Primary English Teaching Association
Laura Street, Newtown NSW 2042 Australia

National Library of Australia Cataloguing-in-Publication data
Beyond the Reading Wars: A balanced approach to helping children learn to read
Edited by Robyn Ewing

Bibliography.
ISBN 1 875622 66 7

1. Reading (Primary). 2. Primary school teaching I. Ewing, Robyn (Robyn Ann), 1955–
II. Primary English Teaching Association (Australia).

372.4

Cover and internal design: Megan Baker
Production editor: Robert Paratore
Printed by Ligare Book Printer, Riverwood
Typeset in Kevlar and Scala Sans

Contents

Acknowledgements

We wish to acknowledge and thank the many teachers, colleagues and students who have contributed to the development of our understandings and ideas, and informed our practices around helping children learn to read. Thank you also to Charles Sturt University and the Universities of Sydney, Western Sydney and Wollongong.

Thank you especially to the Primary English Teaching Association, who saw the need for a book of this nature and accepted it for publication. The production of the book itself was made easier by the expertise and hard work of a number of people. We warmly thank: Robert Paratore for his thoughtful editing; Freya Job, PETA Publications Coordinator, for her excellent coordination of this project; Andrew Connolly, National Coordinator, PETA, for his guidance and advice; Megan Baker, designer extraordinaire; Professor Peter Reimann for the title of the book; David Smith for his close reading and detailed comments about several versions of the manuscript.

We would also like to thank Brendan Smith, Alia Coffey and Belinda and Sarah Cusworth for permission to publish photographs throughout the book.

The authors and publisher acknowledge permission to use extracts from the following sources:

AusAid for permission to reproduce the excerpt on PNG from its website <http://www.ausaid.gov.au> on page 50

The Australian and Samantha Maiden for permission to reproduce the excerpt from 'Report backs literacy basics' by Samantha Maiden (8 December 2005) on page 32

Colin Lankshear for permission to reproduce the excerpt from *Critical literacy, Occasional Paper No. 3* by C. Lankshear on page 142

Australian Literacy Educators Association for permission to reproduce the table from 'Lolly Wrapper Literacy' by Sue Hamilton-Smith in *Literacy Learning in the Middle Years*, Vol. 13, No. 3, October 2005, on page 85

Education Queensland for permission to reproduce the diagram from <http://education.qld.gov.au/corporate/newbasics/> on page 95

Information Age Publishing for permission to reproduce the excerpt from 'What should reading instructional research be research of?' by M. Pressley and R. Allington in *Issues in Education: Contributions for Educational Psychology* 5, 1999, on page 33

International Reading Association (1999) for permission to reproduce the excerpt from *Using multiple methods of beginning reading instruction: A position statement of the International Reading Association* on page 54

Learning Media for permission to reproduce the excerpt from *Meeting of minds* by S. McNaughton on page 70

Lonely Planet Publications for permission to reproduce the excerpt from and the screen grab of <http://www.lonelyplanet.com/worldguide/destinations/pacific/papua-new-guinea/> on pages 50–51

MIT Press for permission to reproduce the excerpt from *Intonation, perception and language* by P. Lieberman on pages 35–36

NSW Department of Education and Training for permission to reproduce the table from *Teaching reading in a multi-age classroom* on page 62

Penguin Group (Australia) and Pamela Allen for permission to reproduce the excerpt from *Grandpa and Thomas* by Pamela Allen on page 47

Phil Cormack, Bill Green and Jo-Anne Reid, authors of the *Schooling Australia* website:
<http://www.unisa.edu.au/cslplc/publications/SchoolingAust_files/homepage.htm>
for permission to reproduce excerpts from:
Education Gazette, August 1922, on page 21
Education, 15 January 1920, on page 18
Education, 15 February 1920, on page 19
Education, 15 September 1928, on page 20

Queensland Studies Authority for permission to reproduce the diagram from *Queensland Years 3, 5 and 7 Literacy and Numeracy Tests Reporting Handbook* on page 93

Routledge Taylor and Francis Group for permission to reproduce excerpts from *Reading images: A grammar of visual design* by G. Kress and T. van Leeuwen on pages 126, 137

Thomson Learning Australia for permission to reproduce the model from *Reading in the primary school years* by P. Harris, J. Turbill, P. Fitzsimmons and B. McKenzie on page 42

About the authors

Derrick Armstrong *University of Sydney*

Derrick Armstrong is Dean of the Faculty of Education and Social Work at the University of Sydney. He is also Co-director of a £1.5m Research Network funded by the UK Economic and Social Research Council investigating young people: *Pathways Into and Out of Crime: Risk, Resilience and Diversity*. The Network centres on a collaboration between five universities in the UK and partners in Australia and the USA. The research is exploring the experiences and perspectives of children and young people in relation to anti-social and criminal behaviour. Before this, he jointly directed the national evaluation of the *On Track* Crime Reduction Programme in the UK, which was concerned with the role of multiple interventions in crime reduction for 6–12 year olds. Other recent projects have included work on the history of special educational policy since 1944, a project on *Self-advocacy, Civil Rights and the Social Model of Disability* and a long-standing interest in special educational assessment and the perspectives of children and parents. A further strand of research over the last ten years, in collaboration with Ann Cheryl Armstrong, has focused on educational development in the Caribbean where he has worked with teachers, NGOs and Education Ministries, and undertaken research funded by the UK's Department for International Development. Derrick is (co)author/editor of 6 books and over 60 articles, book chapters and international conference papers.

Sue Bremner *Association of Independent Schools*

Sue Bremner has been working in the area of specialised ESL and literacy education as a primary teacher and teacher educator for many years. She has worked as a consultant and adviser, writing and delivering professional development for teachers, and producing resources for both teachers and students. Her overall interest is ensuring teaching programs acknowledge what second language learners bring to the literacy classroom.

Brian Cambourne *University of Wollongong*

Brian Cambourne is Associate Professor in the Faculty of Education, University of Wollongong, Australia. Formerly a primary teacher, he entered academia as a teacher educator at Wagga Wagga Teachers' College. He completed his PhD at James Cook University in North Queensland, and was subsequently a Fulbright Scholar and a Post-Doctoral Fellow at Harvard. He has also been a Visiting Fellow at the Universities of Illinois and Arizona. Since 1980, Brian has been researching how learning, especially literacy learning, occurs. He has a strong prejudice that literacy is a cultural resource that enables the less privileged members of any culture to challenge those potentially elitist groups who seek to keep economic and political power for themselves. He also believes that we can only have better, fairer and kinder societies if highly productive, critical literacy is made accessible to as many members of a culture as possible.

Jon Callow *University of Western Sydney*

Jon Callow is a lecturer in literacy education at the University of Western Sydney, Australia. He is an experienced primary teacher, currently teaching tertiary classes in the areas of English, primary literacy and multiliteracies. As a professional literacy consultant, he has worked alongside teachers in their classrooms, both in Australia and the United States. His current interests include visual images and multimodality, the role of multiliteracies in education, and issues of engagement and improved educational outcomes for students from educationally disadvantaged backgrounds.

Ann Daly *NSW Department of Education and Training*

Ann Daly taught in primary classrooms for ten years and then developed statewide literacy assessments for the NSW Department of Education and Training for nine years. During this time Ann completed a Master of Arts in Language and Literacy and used statewide literacy assessment results to carry out research on the relationship between the use of Aboriginal English and literacy achievement. Ann has recently commenced a PhD in Multimodal Literacy Assessment while continuing to work part-time in literacy assessment.

Paul Dufficy *University of Sydney*

Paul Dufficy trained as a primary teacher and then moved into the English as an additional language (EAL) field. He has taught English to children, adolescents and adults in Australia, Pakistan, Thailand and Japan. At present Paul works in the Faculty of Education and Social Work at the University of Sydney where he teaches courses dealing with multilingual classrooms and English as an additional language. He regularly works in classrooms alongside teachers and has a special interest in classroom communication, task-based language development, designing challenging learning, and vocabulary development.

Robyn Ewing *University of Sydney*

For the past 17 years, Robyn Ewing has lectured in curriculum, English, literacy and drama in the Faculty of Education and Social Work at the University of Sydney, and is currently Associate Professor and Associate Dean (Academic Programs). Formerly a primary teacher, she is committed to innovative pedagogy at all levels of education. Robyn believes it is essential to work in close partnership with all members of the profession, especially those in schools. Throughout her career, she has been heavily involved in working as an academic partner alongside teachers interested in transforming their curriculum practices. Robyn's research interests also include the use of drama to enhance the development of critical literacy, quality teaching and learning, the effectiveness of teacher education programs to prepare students for the profession, and the experiences of early career teachers. She was President of the Primary English Teaching Association from 2001 to 2006.

Margery Hertzberg *University of Western Sydney*

Margery Hertzberg trained as a primary teacher and was for many years both an ESL and mainstream teacher in a diverse range of schools. Margery now works at the University of Western Sydney teaching beginning early childhood and primary teachers in literacy, drama and ESL. She has been on the PETA board for three years and is Vice President and Chair of the Professional Development committee. Margery's particular research interest is in how drama can enhance English development, and she works regularly with children and their class teachers in this area.

Clive McArthur *NSW Department of Education and Training*

Clive McArthur qualified as a teacher through the University of Sydney's Master of Teaching Program three years ago. Previously, he spent 16 years in human resources and operations in the corporate world, travelling and working extensively throughout Australia, Asia, New Zealand and the Middle East. He feels the wealth of life experience behind him will greatly assist him to help children who are 'finding their feet' both socially and academically. He is particularly interested in gender issues within the primary arena. He now teaches in suburban Sydney and sits on the PETA board. He also has a science degree, a daughter, and a fish named Otto.

Jo-Anne Reid *Charles Sturt University*

Jo-Anne Reid is Head of the School of Teacher Education at Charles Sturt University and President of the New South Wales Teacher Education Council. She is currently working on two Australian Research Council-funded projects: one investigating the career pathways of Indigenous teachers, the other focused on Literacy in the Environment. She has previously worked on a longitudinal study into the connections between prior-to-school experience and school literacy achievement (*100 Children go to school* and *100 Children turn 10*) and on the *Schooling Australia project: A curriculum history of English teaching, teacher education and public schooling from Federation to World War II*.

Kim Self *NSW Department of Education and Training*

Kim Self is currently an Assistant Principal at an inner-city school in Sydney. She has 17 years' experience teaching in schools with high student populations from non-English speaking backgrounds. Kim is Reading Recovery trained and has worked on DET materials for teaching and assessing literacy, was a district early literacy consultant, and lectured in literacy at UWS.

Alyson Simpson *University of Sydney*

Alyson Simpson is a lecturer in the Faculty of Education and Social Work at the University of Sydney. She lectures in English and literacy in undergraduate and postgraduate primary education programs. Her experience as a teacher librarian led her to investigate new literacies. Her research now focuses on the development of visual literacies through multimodal texts. Part of her work focuses on book raps to examine the pedagogy of online communication as employed in primary classrooms. Alyson is also working on a project that is looking at the development of a metalanguage for visual literacy relevant to K–6.

Bill Spence *NSW Department of Education and Training*

Bill Spence currently manages the production of print and multimedia learning resources for students in New South Wales government schools. He has had many years of experience teaching students in the upper primary years in the western suburbs of Sydney. He strongly believes in the need for students to be supported explicitly in the upper primary years as they access the more complex texts they need to read to meet syllabus requirements across all key learning areas. Bill has been a regional English K–12 consultant, a district literacy consultant and has managed the NSW State Literacy Strategy. He has also lectured in literacy education at undergraduate and postgraduate level at a number of Sydney universities.

Jan Turbill *University of Wollongong*

Jan Turbill is a Senior Lecturer in the Faculty of Education, University of Wollongong, Australia. Her research ranges from early literacy development to the professional development of teachers. More recently she has been researching the use of technology as a support for literacy learning in the early years of schooling and as a medium for professional learning for teachers. She is the author of many books and articles and is President of the Australian Literacy Educators' Association (ALEA).

Robyn Wild *Literacy consultant*

Robyn Wild has worked for the NSW Department of Education and Training as a classroom teacher, assistant principal, literacy consultant, and senior curriculum officer in the Early Learning Unit. Robyn currently works part-time at Macquarie University in the Education Faculty and the Institute of Early Childhood, and at the Universities of Sydney and Wollongong, lecturing on literacy acquisition. Robyn also works as a literacy consultant in schools across New South Wales.

Collaboration involving the diversity of voices seeking reform in literacies is essential. Meeting the literacy expectations of the 21st Century will be achieved not by battle, but by an orchestrated and integrated alliance.

(Fehring, 1999: 274)

Introduction:
A need to move beyond the 'Reading Wars'

> ... there is no single 'essence of reading' that we can spell out and then stamp on each reading event from classroom to classroom, year level to year level, curriculum subject to curriculum subject ...
>
> *(Freebody, 2005: 8)*

Robyn Ewing

In my 30 years as a teacher and teacher educator, no single educational debate in Australian primary education has recurred as often, caused as much angst or been politicised so keenly as that related to the teaching of reading and, more specifically, the merits or disadvantages of using so-called 'whole language' versus 'phonics' methods to help children learn to read.

In late 2004, this damaging and inaccurate polarisation around teaching reading was once more thrust into the public arena when the then-Federal Minister for Education, Brendan Nelson, announced a National Inquiry into the Teaching of Literacy. When the terms of reference were examined, it seemed that the inquiry was really about the teaching of reading, but further scrutiny reduced the focus to centre on those children experiencing difficulty in learning to read. Rather than celebrating the positives and enabling us to look closely at the problems surrounding literacy education in Australia, the subsequent report, *Teaching Reading* (2005), has not moved us forward at all.

In fact, the report takes a highly reductive view of what reading is, defining it in a linear way and stipulating that it *must* start with direct, systematic teaching of phonics. For many of us, learning to read is about much more than decoding: it is about engaging with a text (be it oral, written, visual or electronic) to understand and analyse more than its literal meaning. To do this, our past life experiences, our grasp of the way language is organised, our decoding and predictive skills, and our interpretation of a particular context are all involved. As Eisner (2005) asserts when referring to the US report *No Child Left Behind*, newly conservative trends worldwide seem to have heightened a kind of literacy reductivism when, ironically, the whole notion of what it means to be literate has become increasingly complex.

This book does not pretend there are any ready-made recipes, or answers to perennial problems and debates, but it is our hope that it will be a useful tool for teachers and parents struggling to move beyond the old, damaging battles about the teaching of reading. The book seeks to rebalance the scales for primary and middle school teachers, as well as parents of primary children who need to understand both the current issues and latest research about reading process and pedagogy. Each chapter thus begins with a quote that emphasises this need to look forward. The range of authors involved all have different voices and different approaches, but each author aims to be constructive in addressing the complexity surrounding learning to read in today's society. Some chapters are more theoretical than others, but all relate theory and research to what needs to happen in classrooms. Of course, to focus on reading in isolation is artificial – helping children learn to read needs to be embedded in helping children to be literate more broadly, incorporating talking and listening, reading, writing, and viewing. Time and space constraints have dictated this focus, although there are many references that demonstrate how reading articulates with the other language modes.

In Chapter 1, Derrick Armstrong contextualises the book's raison d'être by providing a passionate critique of the National Inquiry's report, *Teaching Reading*. He raises a number of questions concerned with how we should define literacy in the 21st century, and reminds us that literacy is always a social construction.

In the current context of often bitter debate about reading methods and measurement of children's success against age-standard tests of reading ability, many teachers feel inadequate and exposed, less knowledgeable than they would like to be, and vulnerable to solutions, approaches and strategies that are claimed to ensure success for all their students. To understand how this has played out through generation after generation of Australian teachers, Jo-Anne Reid's chapter tells two moral tales based on research into the history of teaching reading in Australia. In one tale, early in the 20th century, a principal, faced with the task of teaching young children to read in his one-teacher school, devised a method that initially worked so well that a whole education system took it up as the answer to improve the reading performance of all the children in its schools. Other teachers soon came to question this method as failing to provide the promised outcomes, and it was then discounted as worthless and disappeared. Reid demonstrates that, as a profession, we must build and strengthen our practical knowledge base that allows us to *teach children to read* rather than *teach a method of reading.*

In Chapter 3, Brian Cambourne endeavours to help teachers understand the recent reincarnation of the so-called 'reading wars', and the consequent attempts to resurrect and justify the 'explicit and systematic' teaching of phonics as the panacea for ensuring that all pupils achieve adequate levels of literacy. He demonstrates that phonics is an important aspect of literacy learning because it supports learning how to write alphabetic scripts, *not* learning how to read them, and that, while explicitness and systematicity are necessary for the effective teaching of literacy, *they are not sufficient*. Unless explicit, systematic teaching is balanced by high degrees of mindful (as opposed to mindless) teaching, and high degrees of contextualised (as opposed to decontextualised) teaching, learning to read will be more complex than it needs to be.

Chapter 4 revisits the principles around learning to read. Jon Callow and Margery Hertzberg consider what reading means across different contexts and key learning areas (KLAs) using two classroom scenarios. Familiar concepts such as 'cueing systems' and the 'four roles of the reader' are explored, along with the importance of using 'authentic texts'. In Chapter 5, Robyn Wild, Clive McArthur and Kim Self show how to take these concepts and embody them in balanced reading programs in early childhood classrooms. They consider the importance of modelled, guided and independent reading opportunities in every child's reading journey.

In Chapter 6, Paul Dufficy and Sue Bremner highlight aspects of literacy teaching that need to be emphasised for children who are learning English as an additional language (EAL). They outline the often diverse literacy experiences of bilingual children, and suggest some key elements that should underpin our classroom practices, including the need for ongoing oral language development, the importance of culturally inclusive material, the important role of a child's first language, and the need for a wide range of mediational resources.

Assessment for and of learning to read is the focus of Ann Daly's chapter. She includes a range of diagnostic assessment strategies while also exploring ways for students to peer- and self-evaluate their skills in English and literacy. In the shadow of further testing proposals for children in their first year of school, Chapter 7 also briefly examines the benefits and shortcomings of current testing regimes.

Incorporating technology into the early years literacy program has been problematic for teachers for many reasons. In Chapter 8, Jan Turbill examines the need for teachers to change their view of what constitutes literacy in today's world. She draws on her research in primary classrooms to demonstrate how digital cameras and computers can be used to engage teachers and students in reading and writing by using information communication technologies (ICT).

Acquiring reading knowledge and skills is a lifelong process. It is not something that ends when students master the so-called mechanics of reading. To meet the requirements of syllabuses in the middle years, students need to be able to read a wider range of texts for an ever-increasing variety of purposes. In Chapter 9, Bill Spence demonstrates how middle-years students need explicit teaching, guidance and support to increase their repertoire of reading strategies and enable them to deal with the complexities of these texts.

Alyson Simpson approaches the topic of visual literacy in Chapter 10. She takes the view that children need to know how to read images, not just look at them. A deep understanding of visual texts enables the viewer to move beyond the everyday acceptance of seeing/reading images at a surface level. Her case study material illustrates how teachers working with picture books and factual texts can encourage children to 'talk out' images.

The final chapter encourages teachers to help children read beyond text. It draws on continuing work with primary teachers and children in a diverse range of Sydney classrooms to demonstrate how valuable drama can be in helping children transcend the technical or 'basic/operational' (Rowan, 2005), using their already rich imaginations to read and understand the multiple meanings and perspectives of contemporary children's literature.

In a newly conservative, highly technical and often reductive climate, it is tempting to grasp hold of a ready-made, step-by-step approach to teaching reading if it promises to be the answer for every child. The complexities that exist around learning to be literate in the 21st century continue to increase and cannot be understated. As a group of concerned educators, we do not claim to have all the answers, but it is our intention to demonstrate constructive ways to move forward. While we are all aware that there is still much about literacy and the reading process that we don't understand, it is important that we don't lose heart. We need to have faith in our creativity, as well as our understandings and capabilities, in order to continue to meet the diverse needs of our students.

References

Department of Education, Science and Training (DEST) (2005) *Teaching Reading: Report and Recommendations.* National Inquiry into the Teaching of Literacy. Canberra: Commonwealth of Australia.

Eisner, E. (2005) Teaching for artistic behaviour. Keynote address. National Arts Education Association Conference, Boston, March.

Fehring, H. (1999) Influences on teachers' judgements of students' literacy development in a Victorian context. Unpublished Doctor of Philosophy thesis, RMIT, Melbourne.

Freebody, P. (2005) Hindsight and foresight: Putting the four roles model of reading to work in the daily business of teaching. In A. Healy & E. Honan (Eds), *Text next: New resources for literacy learning.* Sydney: Primary English Teaching Association.

Rowan, L. (2005) 'Journeying towards literacy: Are we there yet?' *Occasional paper 1.* Sydney: Primary English Teaching Association.

we need to hold expectations of excellence in acquiring literacy for all children.

(McNaughton, 2002:7)

1 Future directions in literacy[1]

Derrick Armstrong

This is a very timely book, published at a time when there is considerable public and policy interest in the teaching of language and literacy skills, prompted in no small part by the recent publication of the report of the National Inquiry into the Teaching of Literacy, *Teaching Reading* (DEST, 2005a).

Much comment on teacher education and the teaching of literacy has focused attention on supposed inadequacies in the way that universities prepare new teachers for teaching literacy skills in the classroom. At its worst, such criticism has resurrected tired old complaints that a sound grounding in phonics has been usurped by a 'woolly', and perhaps politically motivated, emphasis upon 'constructivism'. Practice in this area has long since moved on, and the importance of an integrated and multi-method approach to the teaching of reading is widely recognised by teachers and teacher educators. In this respect, the National Inquiry into the Teaching of Literacy is struggling to catch up with what is already happening in teacher education and in schools across the country. On the

---

[1] This chapter is adapted from Professor Armstrong's opening address at the Future Directions in Literacy Conference, University of Sydney, 3–4 March 2006.

other hand, the Inquiry does, mostly by default, raise some issues that are worth spending time considering.

John Willinsky (1998) in his book *Learning to divide the world* retells the story of Frederick Douglas and his education as a slave in America. Douglas described his surreptitious acquisition of literacy by tricking white children into sharing the letters of the alphabet with him. As he acquired the ability to read and write, he experienced, as he put it, "a new and special revelation" about the nature of slavery: "I now understand what has been for me a most perplexing difficulty – to wit the white man's power to enslave the black man ... From that moment I understood the pathway from slavery to freedom". Willinsky argues that not only does this statement affirm a fundamental faith in learning; it also affirms the power of reading and writing in enforcing the superiority of whites over blacks. Although Douglas appears delighted with stealing the secret of fire from the gods, his statement also suggests the moral hollowness of those whose authority is based on inscribing letters on a page. Whatever education's complicity with power, Douglas turns it against that power and into something to be prized as it liberates.

It is in this sense that debates about literacy, and in particular the teaching of reading, go to the heart of the role and place of education in our society. Without question, learning to read involves the mastery of technical skills. Just as Douglas needed to learn, even by surreptitious means, the letters of the alphabet, learning to read involves: phonemic awareness, phonics, fluency, vocabulary knowledge, and text comprehension. As the report of the National Inquiry into the Teaching of Literacy argues: "The evidence is clear ... that direct, systematic instruction in phonics during the early years of schooling is an essential foundation for teaching children to read" (DEST, 2005: 11).

As teacher educators, if we didn't take this evidence, and these skills, seriously we would be doing a grave disservice both to beginning teachers and to the educational interests of future generations. Very few people I have talked to or heard commenting in the media, and none in teacher education, have questioned the importance of the Inquiry's findings in this respect. Indeed, many would argue that, for the most part, the report merely affirms the practice of teachers of language and literacy in our schools, and also supports the practice of teacher educators. Yet, it misses an opportunity to affirm the wider significance of literacy in our society; that is, in the relationship between literacy and democratic participation, and it does this democracy a disservice by failing to acknowledge the social context and significance of illiteracy.

Too much of the literacy debate 'forgets'; it forgets the complexity of our histories and how, as for Frederick Douglas, these histories position us in relation to knowledge, informing our understanding and use of skills. To uncritically read the report of the National Inquiry is to assume that learners come to education free from prior experiences and independent of the histories of their communities and families.

The concept of 'evidence-based teaching' is flashed around as though it provides solutions to all problems, but the nature of 'evidence' is itself so often selective, so often tuned to particular ways of seeing the world and interpretations of the experiences, needs and aspirations of different individuals and communities. Evidence inevitably stands in a relationship to values (if only in terms of what questions are asked), and assessments of evidence should be understood in relation to an exploration of the values that such evidence foregrounds.

The first piece of evidence of note that is referred to by the Inquiry report, before being quickly cast aside, is that "15-year-old students in Australian schools perform notably better than the majority of their counterparts in other OECD countries" (DEST, 2005a: 26). This is no mean achievement! Perhaps something for which our teachers and our teacher educators might reasonably expect some praise. But, no, we will not find it here. We are instead presented with three further studies that proclaim, despite this first piece of evidence, that there really is a problem in the teaching of literacy.

A 1997 study by the Australian Bureau of Statistics found that approximately 20% of Australians aged 15 to 74 were identified as having "very poor literacy skills". Putting aside the rather complex question of whether or not agreed definitions of literacy are being used in the definition of the problem, what this 10-year-old study shows (the data was gathered in 1996) is that 20% of Australians who attended schools between 1926 and 1996 have poor literacy skills. Of course, it is quite likely that a significant number of these did not receive their education in Australia at all. Moreover, we might reasonably expect that for some English would be their second language. Regardless of these considerations, it is doubtful that teachers and teacher educators in today's schools and universities can be held responsible for the literacy difficulties experienced by those born in the 1920s, 1930s and so on.

Two further studies are quoted in the report in support of the view that there is a crisis in Australian literacy education. Unfortunately, the evidence from each of these two studies contradicts the other. Thus the National School English Literacy Survey from 1996 suggested that 27% of Year 3 and 29% of Year 5 students did not meet the minimum performance standards of literacy required for effective participation in further schooling. Again, this evidence is 10 years old, but bear with me because the second piece of evidence that is quoted (MCEETYA, 2005) is far more recent and shows that, in 2003, 8% of Year 3 and 11% of Years 5 and 7 students were not achieving national benchmarks for reading. In other words, there appears to have been a significant improvement in literacy standards in our schools over a 7-year period!

But once again, instead of teachers and teacher educators being applauded for their success, we are told that "these outcomes are unacceptable". Indeed we shouldn't accept them, but at least let the high levels of literacy in our schools be acknowledged, and let us acknowledge the contribution of teachers and teacher educators to the achievement and continual improvement of these high standards.

The Inquiry report is accompanied by a whole booklet that goes under the title *Literature Review* (DEST, 2005b). Unfortunately, for a document that places such an emphasis upon 'evidence-based teaching', the evidence contained in this document is rather sparse. Perhaps most disappointing is the admission on page 5 that: "Due to uncertainty about operational definitions of *learning difficulties* and *reading difficulties* ... it is difficult to provide authoritative estimates of the proportion of children who have such difficulties". It might be argued that if there are operational difficulties in defining these terms, then how can we have any certainty about the methods of teaching literacy that are appropriate for addressing such difficulties. But there is something else that worries me about the argument put forward regarding this lack of clarity about definitions.

A footnote on page 5 comments that: "... an explication of the underlying 'causes' of such difficulties are beyond the remit of the present review ... However, factors contributing to such difficulties include: socio economic and cultural impoverishment, indigenous status, neuro-physiological and psycho-behavioural factors, as well as inadequate and/or inappropriate teaching and learning provision". We are not told what proportion of the population with difficulties can be attributed to each of these factors or what evidence there is to support the claim that these factors are relevant or significant in the first place. What is apparent is that the report accepts that inadequate and/or inappropriate teaching, at the very worst, can account for only a proportion of the difficulties experienced by what in the first place is only a relatively small number of children. Yet endlessly the finger is pointed at teachers and teacher educators as a culture of blame is whipped up.

I could only speculate on what the agenda of the authors of this shoddy report might be. But their own use of language is telling. For instance, I am intrigued by what they mean by 'cultural impoverishment'. Was Frederick Douglas 'culturally impoverished' or did his lack of reading skills result from the institutionalised racism and socio economic exploitation of slavery? Was his 'new and special revelation' that enabled him to understand 'the white man's power to enslave the black man' the outcome of a phonetic road to Damascus? And in what sense is 'indigenous status' a cause of illiteracy? Are we to understand that Indigenous people are to blame for their own poverty and degradation in Australian history, or that when they achieve high standards of educational achievement they have overcome their own 'impoverished culture'? (Which is another way of saying 'they become like us'.)

In other ways, the report of the National Inquiry is not as controversial as some of the hype would have us believe. Many of its recommendations are already firmly embedded in 'good practice', if not in the dogmatic and one-sided way that the report advocates. In other respects, the report is a sad, soulless document that says nothing about the conditions of social variation that ought to command our attention. It is a report that advocates a technical solution to an ill-defined problem. It leaves many questions unanswered and not considered important enough to reflect upon.

1. Who has problems with learning to read?
2. What does their experience say, not only about the problem of illiteracy, but about social and economic participation and the nature of 'citizenship' in our society?
3. How is the problem of illiteracy represented? What agendas are pursued by framing problems and solutions in particular ways?
4. What is the value of reading, and how are teaching methods related to the ways in which this value is understood?
5. What assumptions about social participation underpin different approaches to reading and learning to read?

One of the saddest things about the report is the way it harks back to a glorious linguistic past when correct English was defined by rules handed down to us by our social superiors. This 'glorious past', of course, was never a reality. As Raymond Williams (1961) pointed out, it was perhaps Dr Johnson who first expounded the doctrine that the spelling of a word is the best guide to its pronunciation, yet such a standard was largely an artificial creation based on false premises. As Williams would, I am sure, have added if he had been invited to make a submission to the National Inquiry into the Teaching of Literacy, "The habits of language are too strong to be wholly altered by determined yet relatively ignorant teachers [such as the authors of this report], but the mark of their effort is still with us, and the tension they create is still high". Not only is English spelling an extremely unreliable guide to pronunciation, but the very notion of correct pronunciation is embedded in attempts to enforce the social superiority of some groups over others. The history of the living language, by contrast, tells of another story. Paradoxically, as Gunther Kress (2003) has argued, now, "at the very time when language is escaping the control of those who previously had been able to (deceive themselves that they could) legislate in this way", the insistence on rules for the transliteration of letters into sounds (phonics) has once more raised its head as the gospel for teaching reading. But there are too many real problems for such an approach to have any credibility as the sole or even principal method for teaching reading, despite its value as one among a number of strategies. It is quite impossible, as Kress argues, to settle on one form of English as standard. Moreover, some reflection on the colonial histories of the uses and misuses of language in the creation of difference as 'cultural deprivation' might, in Australia, give us some pause for thought.

What gratifies me about this book is that the writers are clearly aware of and engaged in a much wider discussion of the meaning, importance and pursuit of literacy in the context of democratic participation. Hopefully, their voices will be heard above the dull reductionism and the historical indifference that some would place as constraints around Frederick Douglas's idea of literacy as creating opportunities for 'new and special revelation'.

References

Department of Education, Science and Training (DEST) (2005a) *Teaching Reading: Report and Recommendations.* National Inquiry into the Teaching of Literacy. Canberra: Commonwealth of Australia.

Department of Education, Science and Training (DEST) (2005b) *Teaching Reading: Literature Review. A review of the evidence-based research literature on approaches to the teaching of literacy, particularly those that are effective in assisting students with reading difficulties.* National Inquiry into the Teaching of Literacy. Canberra: Commonwealth of Australia.

Kress, G. (2003) *Literacy in the new media age.* London: Routledge.

MCEETYA (2005) *National Report on Schooling in Australia 2003, Preliminary paper, National Benchmark results for Reading, Writing and Numeracy, Years 3, 5 and 7.* Canberra: Ministerial Council on Education, Employment, Training and Youth Affairs.

McNaughton, S. (2002) *Meeting of minds.* Wellington, New Zealand: Learning Media.

Williams, R. (1961) *The long revolution.* London: Chatto & Windus.

Willinsky, J. (1998) *Learning to divide the world: Education at the empire's end.* Minneapolis: University of Minnesota Press.

None of the responsibilities for ensuring the appropriate conditions for learning to read can be met by experts or authorities outside the classroom. The conditions can't be prepackaged in commercialised kits of learning materials, electronic or otherwise. And the conditions certainly can't be mandated by any kind of legislation.

(Smith, 1999:6)

2 Reading stories: Understanding our professional history as teachers of reading

Jo-Anne Reid

In my family, the history is that I could read when I was two – only one book, unfortunately, *The Polka Dot Tots* – which probably explains why I kept my fascination with the Bobbsey Twins way past an age when it could have been considered healthy. My children all read early too, and I remember being satisfied that my ideal of raising a politically conscious generation might be easily reached when Caroline demanded to know, aged two herself, why "all those goats crossing that high bridge" were boys and "where was the girl goat?". I very quickly learned to mount a feminist critique of the fairytales we read each night as she railed against the absence or subordination of little girls in the Noddy books or *The Magic Faraway Tree*.

I first started noting that things were changing when her younger brother, Andrew, asked a slightly different question at three. He enjoyed reading too, but equally enjoyed sitting with his big brother playing Nintendo, and taping favourite TV programs such as *The Simpsons* to watch over and over again, in the same way he read his books. He looked up from the television set, on which was playing a lilting old black-and-white Danny Kaye movie, and asked, "Mum, were you born before the world turned to colour?" I suddenly realised that reading the visual text was fundamentally different from reading a print text – the parameters of assumed reality were far more structured for the viewer, and a feminist (and/or any other ideological) critique was insufficient to allow Andrew access to understanding the technological and filmic conventions of the visual text. Andrew is now nineteen, and claims not to remember that conversation ... even though he was just as much in it as I was. History, it seems (even these minor histories within our families), is very much a matter of who is telling the story, and who is reading it.

In a context of often bitter debate about reading methods, and the success of children against age-standard tests of reading ability, many teachers are made to feel inadequate and exposed, less knowledgeable than they would like to be, and vulnerable to tried-and-true solutions, approaches and strategies that are claimed to guarantee success in reading for their pupils. To understand how this tension has played out through generation after generation of schoolteachers, I will tell two stories based on research into the history of the teaching of reading in Australia. One shows how a teacher, faced with the task of teaching young children in his one-teacher school, devised a method that worked so well that a whole education system took it up as the answer to improve the reading performance of all the children in its schools. The other story tells how this method came into question as failing to provide the outcomes it promised, and how it was then discounted as worthless and disappeared.

This chapter shows what went wrong in each case, and what we can learn from our history as a profession to build and strengthen a practical knowledge base that allows us to teach children to read, rather than teaching a method of reading. I have begun with these stories of my own because I want to stress the point of this chapter from the very beginning – the teaching of reading must be constantly changing and adapting, in order to meet the needs of the children for whom we are responsible, the purposes to which they put their reading skills, and the materials and technologies that produce the things that are to be read at any particular time and place. There is never one right way that we can rely on, as teachers, to be 'all we need'. To argue this point, I take the example of a reading method that was once touted in NSW as the best way to teach reading to all children, and show how this very successful method was first of all taken up, but then very quickly called into question as not actually doing the job it promised.

This reading approach was called the Jones Method, and I have told this story elsewhere (Reid & Green, 2004) in a more formal and detailed account. Here, I want to explain first of all what the Jones Method was, and then show how teachers came to find that it was not enough to solve the 'problem' of teaching reading.

Story One: A wonderful new method ...

About a hundred years ago, a phonics-based approach called the Ellis Method was taught to teachers as the most efficient way of teaching reading (Reid & Green, 2004). It was successful in helping children learn to sound out their letters, but a 1922 critique of it claimed that:

> 1. The method does not follow the natural development of perception, as it begins with elements in themselves meaningless to the children, and proceeds to combine them into words.
> 2. The method is so logical that it is practically an adult method ... [and] entails an amount of reasoning that is foreign to the child's stage of development.
> 3. The early reading is so restricted that it is very hard to awaken interest in the child.
> 4. It has the disadvantage of other phonetic methods based on a differentiation of type. The child has to examine the word so closely that it is likely to affect his eyesight.
>
> *(Archibald, 1922)*

The Ellis Method relied on intensive drilling of sound–letter correspondences, and it appears that it had caused teachers and students both to lose interest in the teaching of reading and to ignore the other important roles of a reader (Freebody & Luke, 1990), beyond simple decoding of text. Teachers needed a new way of teaching phonics that would address this issue, and, as Archibald (1922: 181) wrote, the arrival of a new method: "[i]n which the elements of words were introduced in a play way, was received with relief".

This new method was devised by George Jones, who was Principal at Bundarra Public School in the north-west of NSW. He had been in this one-teacher school for 25 years, and during that time had worked to perfect the design of a method of teaching reading that was not boring or disengaging for him or his pupils. As Jones (1920: 9) wrote:

> The phonetic deficiencies and difficulties of the English alphabet have always made the teaching of Reading a task rather than a pleasure, particularly in the initial stages. [A]ny system, to be effective, must be full of interest, impressive and simple. These are points of value claimed for this system which is phonographic, but does not in any way interfere with or alter the characters of the existing alphabet.

When the Inspector for the region compared the oral reading of the children at Bundarra with that of children taught by other teachers, Mr Jones's method began to be seen as a great success. In an invited address to the NSW Teachers' Federation Annual Conference in 1919, Jones demonstrated his system of teaching reading. The report of the session allows us some insight into the reasoning behind his method:

> He [Jones] had come to the conclusion that the fault lay with the mother tongue, which was full of phonic difficulties. In order to make it thoroughly phonetic he sat down night after night and formulated a new alphabet. That alphabet consisted of letters and signs. There were 19 vowels, 16 consonants and one silent letter in the alphabet. [...] Anyone could take it up with the use of the chart and the necessary notes for their guidance. The child must feel that it was interested. The fault in the past lay not with the child, but with the system.
>
> *(Education, 15 January 1920: 66)*

The Jones Method was complicated in this sense. But it was consistent, and as Jones (1920: 1, emphasis added) wrote:

> ... a new alphabet had to be formed, of which each symbol was to represent one of the sounds of standard English. Only unmarked letters carried their intrinsic value, in all other cases *the sign not the letter indicated the sound.*

Its key difference from the Ellis Method, for teachers, was that it involved the children in hand movements, which paralleled the special diacritical marking of the words they were learning to read.

> The children first make a 'sound' in their hands. For example, the long sound of **i** is represented by the hands being placed together at the tips of the fingers, and then coming down in a tent shape, the letter **m** is shown by the hands being placed horizontally together. The combination of these two hand movements gives the word 'my'. The various vowel sounds are arranged in progressions, which have a certain similarity of movement. In this way the children associate sounds and hand movements.
>
> The next step is to associate these sounds with diacritical marks, which bear a close resemblance to the hand play, e.g. **i** is shown by the diacritical mark ʌ. Which resembles the tent shape previously made by the hands. The next step in association is connecting the diacritical mark with its letter equivalent, e.g. ʌ may be written as **i**, **igh**, or **y**. A favourite exercise with the children is that of 'dressing' the signs, e.g. the following would be written on the blackboard:
>
> + + + +
> **d n h s   b t**
>
> and the children would write the corresponding words underneath:
>
> + + + +
> **dan has a bat**
>
> In this way the children obtain a familiarity with words in [an] easy and pleasant way.
>
> *(Archibald, 1922: 181)*

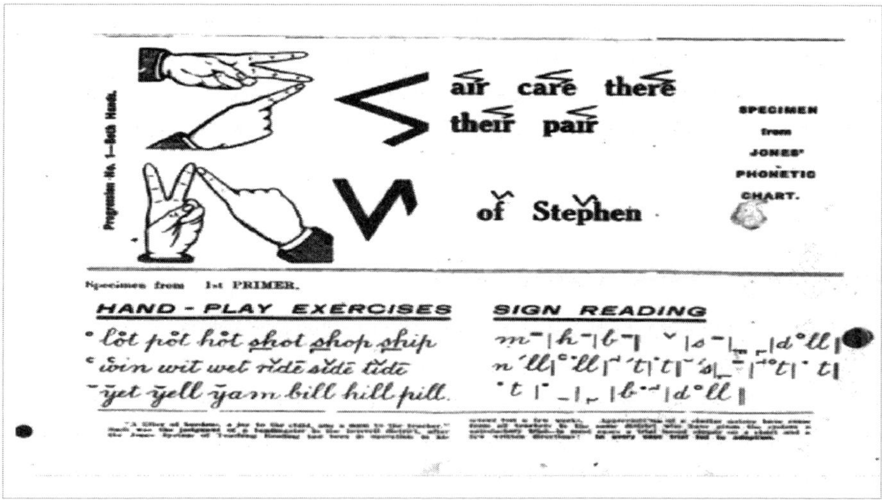

Figure 1: Illustration of hand positions for the Jones Method

Jones's method attracted attention from within the Education Department, and was sponsored by several Inspectors who recommended his work. As reported in Reid and Green (2004), what had begun in 1918 – when "intense enthusiasm" had gripped "Bundarra on the Gwydir", and "teachers for thirty miles around assembled to hear Mr Jones explain his method of teaching to read" (*Education*, 15 May 1920: 168) – took hold of the educational imagination of the time. Eighteen months later, Jones and his publisher were advertising a Summer School at Fort Street (*Education*, 15 December 1921: 21). From 1920 he worked in Sydney so that "the many more teachers of the metropolitan district" (*Education*, 15 May 1920: 168) could gain professional development in this method.

Part of the reason for the success of the Jones Method seemed to lie in the help it provided to both the child and the teacher. Jones claimed that: "The child becomes self-active, self-reliant, and finds out how to sound words for itself. Thus the teacher finds that the irksome stage of elementary teaching of Reading has lost its boredom" (*Education*, 15 February 1920: 92). For the teacher, though, the benefits were far more pragmatic:

> Besides being of great value in the kindergarten and infant classes, there is a special value to be placed upon it in schools of one teacher. In such the attention of the teacher is diverted owing to so many classes needing aid. As a preparatory aid to a new Reading lesson, the diacritics are marked where necessary, and as these enable the pupils to pronounce the words for themselves, the lesson is learned by silent reading, and the thought content arrived at while the teacher is engaged elsewhere. This is a claim of precious value to such teachers as well as to the children.
>
> (Education, *15 February 1920: 93)*

We may well ask, however, what happened to the Jones Method over the rest of the century. If it was such a successful method of teaching children to read, and so useful to teachers in classroom control and management, why did it not last as a preferred method? Where did it fail? What critiques could be made of it? This is the focus of the second story.

A shorter story: What came next ...

It seems that the Jones Method, after a bright flourishing in the mid-1920s, all but disappeared from Departmental documents and advertisements in *Education* and *The Gazette*. Certainly, in the following years, we could find no more advertisements for the method, although by this time it was significantly well known among teacher educators, and student teachers were informed about this method. In our research into this subject (Green, Cormack & Reid, 2000), we did find one person who remembers being taught to read by the Jones Method, in a small school near Inverell in the late 1930s, and Jones's books remained on the reading lists at Armidale Teachers' College into the mid-1930s. Articles and materials in *Education* over this period focused on the teaching of writing, and articles about reading disappeared for a year or so, with the introduction by the Department of a new simplified cursive handwriting style, and increasing attention to spelling.

But then, as noted in Reid and Green (2004), by 1928, a practising teacher ('Teacher 139') suggested there was a link between the teaching of reading and success in spelling. This teacher also suggested that poor teaching was responsible for the poor spelling of students:

> I would like to state that I have heard sound teachers of nearly thirty years' experience express the opinion that they cannot achieve the results that they formerly obtained. I know that it is not due to any falling off in enthusiasm on their part, nor yet lack of effective methods. But I believe that, unconsciously, many of them have suffered from the effects of pinning their faith too closely to a particular method of teaching reading, forgetting that none is perfect.
>
> (Education, *15 September 1928: 358)*

Teacher 139's comments ring true to our situation today:

> During the past fifteen years or so, we have had a rich crop of methods for teaching reading, none of which I wholly condemn, but I cannot help thinking that teachers have not always understood the principle underlying the methods adopted, and floundering as one learning to swim, they have not achieved the results which the author or an enthusiastic exponent of that method can and does achieve.
>
> (Education, *15 September 1928: 358)*

The vernacular understanding of 'reading', at this time, was still very much reading aloud. Miss Archibald, writing in the *Education Gazette* as a respected Infants Mistress, expressed a wider view of reading. She proposed that the following criteria should be considered in judging a 'packaged' reading method before teachers chose to implement it in their classrooms:

> 1. Does it create from the beginning a definite connection between the child's spoken language, with which he is already familiar, and the new written language he is now attempting to learn for the first time?
> 2. Is it sufficiently elastic to allow of the introduction of a certain amount of motor activity in the early stages?
> 3. Is it so planned that very soon the emphasis may be placed on the real aim of reading, viz. thought getting, and so a love of reading be fostered in the children?
> 4. Does it provide a means for the mastery of the mechanical difficulties of reading?
>
> *(Archibald, 1922: 179)*

While the Jones Method appeared to score well on most of these criteria, it became increasingly obvious that, in the hands of many teachers, it failed in terms of helping children get beyond the sounding of words to the 'real aim of reading'. It is interesting to compare Archibald's criteria with Freebody's (2001: 2) list of "four sets of considerations that need to be dealt with in the use of commercial early-literacy packages":

- What view of reading and writing is the package based on?
- Are there additional learnings or skills needed for children to master the material?
- How consistent is the package with classroom practice?
- How does the package respond to the needs of individual children?

As one of the first commercial literacy packages available to teachers in Australia, the Jones Method was certainly susceptible to critique on some of these grounds too. While it was consistent with the needs of Mr Jones's classroom practice, and did respond to the demonstrated needs of his beginning readers to have lots of practice and to be more physically involved in learning to sound out their words, the children did need to learn additional skills in order to be able to learn the original skills that the method aimed to teach. Further, the view of reading that it was based on, and its value in teaching spelling and writing, was clearly limited. Like all methods that might appear to be the salvation of the teacher, it, too, was not enough.

Reading methods: A means to an end

I started this chapter with two anecdotes about my own children learning to read, and have argued, through the stories of the rise and fall of the Jones Method for teaching reading, that there is never one right way that we can rely on, as teachers, to help us succeed in this task. The teaching of reading must constantly change and adapt to meet the needs of the children we teach, the purposes to which they put their reading skills, and the materials and technologies that produce the things that are to be read.

Mr Jones's reading scheme used up-to-date technology to provide interesting and relevant visual materials for the children who were learning to read in classrooms around New South Wales in the 1920s. Children today have a much wider range of experiences, many of which are mediated by technology, to bring to the work of learning to read. And, often, a reliance and focus on print text in early reading classrooms may no longer be the most appropriate means for children to learn.

I want to conclude with another two stories, to underline this point. Both are about young readers in their first year at school being taught to read by another method that has caught the attention of teachers around Australia. Its similarities to Mr Jones's method are clear, although there are also several differences – first of which is the fact that this method does not require the children to learn one set of skills before they can learn to sound their letters. For the child in the first story, the teaching is not working. For the other, it has suddenly 'clicked'.

My next-door neighbour, Lisa, said the other day that Rowan, her second born, has not taken well to preschool. His big brother, Morgan, had raced open eyed and open hearted into the preschool classroom that Lisa had chosen for him, played busily with the sand and water and wooden blocks, and listened enthralled to the stories that the teacher read each morning, lunch and afternoon, soaking up all that she could provide for him. Rowan, by contrast, has not enjoyed the curriculum on offer in the same teacher's classroom two years later.

Lisa is concerned. Rowan sometimes does not want to go to school, and is often fretful over his breakfast and dressing, so that the morning rush to school is becoming a chore. This morning he declared flatly that he "hates those jolly phonics!". Lisa has sought my advice. What can she do for her little boy? Why has his teacher's classroom changed so markedly between the experience that was provided for Morgan and that which Rowan experiences? Rowan used to read Morgan's storybooks every afternoon before he started school – after *Rug Rats* and before *Power Rangers*. Now he shows little interest in reading with his brother, and only reads with Lisa when she sits with the boys at bedtime or after their baths. Somehow, Rowan has failed to make the connection between the reading and viewing that he does know how to enjoy and find pleasure in, and the method his teacher is using to teach him to read.

The second story is based on a train trip home from Sydney, where, at Granville, a young family pushed the baby's pram through the aisle of the carriage to where I was sitting, and three little children clambered around me. "Hey, Lady!" offered wide-eyed Hope. "Hey, Lady, we goin' to Daddy's house! We goin' to Lithgow!" Her brothers looked warily at me, and then smiled when I did. "Yep," said Adam, in his new school uniform, "all the way to Lithgow." John, who didn't seem able to talk yet, mumbled "Dad", and the baby, Dean, kicked his feet in the pram so that John could grab one to pull. For the next two hours I watched Adam learning to read as the train roared through the western suburbs towards their weekend at Dad's.

It began with a predictable "Are we there yet?" question, to which his mother said, "No, here we are at Blacktown, see the sign?" And Adam did. "Blacktown", "Mount Druitt", "St Marys", his mother read to him as we rolled through the next few stations. "Next stop Penrith," came the voice of the guard over the loudspeaker. Adam read "Penrith" himself. And then, as the train began to stop at the stations on the Western line, he worked his way up the mountains through Glenwood, Warrimoo, Faulconbridge and Hazelbrook, testing out the guard's advice on the platform signs. It's a long five minutes between Bullaburra and Wentworth Falls, and Dean was getting rambunctious as Hope started singing "The wheels on the truck ..." from *Play School*, in time with the rhythm of the train. Adam stood up on the seat and noticed the sign on the carriage wall: "Please vacate this seat for old or infirm passengers". He looked up and then back at his sister, whose song was finishing. He caught her eye, and pointed to the sign.

> "Dolphins diving, d. d. d.
>
> Dolphins diving, d. d. d.
>
> Dolphins diving, d. d. d
>
> And that's the sound that 'D' makes!"

As he sang and made 'dolphins diving' movements with his arms, his mother joined in. So did Hope, while little John stood beside the pram holding onto Dean's waving foot once again, bobbing up and down. Adam was in charge of the sign, now. He missed Wentworth Falls, and Leura, as he worked through the letters in the sign, singing the phonics jingle he had been learning at school, to entertain his brothers and sister. His teacher would have loved to see Adam loving the letters and the words he was able to make out in the collections of letters on the sign. When he looked out of the window again, he had missed the guard's announcement in the middle of a song, and saw the station approaching. "Ka...toom...ba," he read. "Katoomba! We are nearly up the mountains!"

What is different about reading for Rowan and Adam here is the point that Miss Archibald made back in 1922. Unless the experience of reading can "awaken interest in the child", it will not succeed – regardless of the method the teacher chooses to use. For this is what reading is about: the realisation that you can get information, or pleasure, from print, or from a video, or an advertisement, that allows you to take charge of the activity yourself. Mr Jones's pupils did get enough pleasure and power from the method he designed for them to want to continue to read the materials he provided in his classroom, but this did not happen for other children, with other teachers, who saw the 'method' as an end in itself, rather than a means to an end. In their home environment, both Caroline and Andrew experienced the power of reading that enabled them to question the reality presented in the print and video texts they read and enjoyed. And Adam was able to relate the phonics instruction he was getting at school to the letters on the sign, thus making the railway station signs his own growing source of information as he catalogued his family's train journey, and taught himself the meaning of reading. Poor Rowan, however, has not yet been able to see a purpose for reading. With any luck, though, his teacher understands that the 'jolly phonics' method that Rowan is already tired of is not enough on its own to enable him to learn to read either powerfully or with pleasure.

References

Archibald, J. (1922) 'A survey of reading methods and an account of the reconciliation of the Jones Method (synthetic) with the word and sentence methods (analytic)', *Education Gazette*, August: 1–6.

Education (1920) Record of the 1919 New South Wales Teachers' Federation Annual Conference, 15 January, p. 66.

Education (1920) 'The Jones System of Teaching Reading', 15 February, pp. 92–93.

Education (1920) 'The Jones System of Teaching', 15 May, p. 168.

Education (1921) 'Jones Reading System: Summer school', 15 December, p. 21.

Education (1928) 'Spelling in the primary school', 15 September, p. 58.

Freebody, P. (2001) 'Crafting a mix: Programs and packages in literacy education'. Accessed 30/3/06 at: <http://www.alea.edu.au/crafting.htm>

Freebody, P., & Luke, A. (1990) 'Literacies programs: Debates and demands in cultural context'. *Prospect*, 5(3): 7–16.

Green, B., Cormack, P., & Reid, J. (2000) 'Learning from our past ...' *English in Australia*, No. 127-128, May: 111–119.

Jones, G. E. (1920) *The Jones System of Reading*. Sydney: G. B. Philip & Son Publishers.

Jones, G. E. (n.d.) *The Jones System of Reading: First primer*. Sydney: G. B. Philip & Son Publishers.

Luke, A. (1998) 'Getting over method: Literacy teaching as work in "New Times" '. *Language Arts*, 75(4): 305–313.

Reid, J., & Green, B. (2004) 'Displacing method(s)? Historical perspective in the teaching of reading'. *Australian Journal of Language and Literacy*, February, Vo1. 1: 12–26.

Smith, F. (1999) 'Why systematic phonics and phonemic awareness instruction constitute an educational hazard'. *Language Arts*, 77(2): 150–155.

...reading is not an activity that can be divided into developmental bits and taught one bit at a time. It is a social practice that must be engaged in in it's entirety in a sympathetic and supportive environment in which the purpose is made clear and the focus is on meaning.

(Green, 2003: 123)

Playing 'Chinese whispers' with the pedagogy of literacy

Brian Cambourne

Introduction

'Chinese whispers' (also known as 'Broken telephone' and 'Whisper down the line') is a well-known classroom listening activity. A number of players line up so that they can whisper to their immediate neighbours but not hear any players farther away. The player at the 'beginning' of the line thinks of a phrase (or, in the case of young children, is supplied with one by the teacher), and whispers it as quietly as possible to their neighbour. The neighbour then passes on the message to the next player, to the best of their ability. The message is passed in this fashion until it reaches the player at the 'end' of the line, who calls out the message they received. While the intent of the game is to pass the message intact down to the end of the line, typically the final message bears little or no resemblance to the original, due to the cumulative effect of mistakes along the line. Teacher and students usually laugh at the changes that occur between the first and the last message, and most teachers use the opportunity to help their students understand the roles that clear speech and careful listening play in interpretation. (Adapted from Wikipedia, 2006.)

So what's 'Chinese whispers' got to do with the National Inquiry into the Teaching of Literacy?

While at first glance comparing the recommendations in the report of the National Inquiry into the Teaching of Literacy to the 'Chinese whispers' game might seem 'forced', from another perspective it can be both interesting and informative.

Let me explain why. *Teaching Reading*, the report of the National Inquiry into the Teaching of Literacy (DEST, 2005), makes 20 recommendations related to the teaching of reading in Australian schools. Of these 20 recommendations, only one (Recommendation 2) speaks *directly* to primary teachers. The other 19 are aimed at groups that are gradually more remote from primary classrooms. Working backwards from the classroom, there are recommendations aimed at:

- state and federal education departmental administrators who make these policies (and who also control the budgets for those further down the chain);
- school leaders charged with implementing departmental policy;
- university staff who teach pre-service teacher education courses; and,
- secondary school subject specialists.

In some ways, these groups are similar to the players in a game of 'Chinese whispers'. The authors of the report are like the teacher who gives the phrase to the player at the beginning of the line, while the classroom teachers are like the players at the other end.

At this point the analogy begins to break down, but not before it begins to throw some light on the possible implications of this Inquiry for teachers. For example, unlike the classroom version of 'Chinese whispers', the authors of the report do *not* expect the information in their message to be distorted or changed. Nor do they expect us all to have a hearty chuckle at the differences between the original and the final message(s). Rather, their intention is just the opposite. They want to ensure that the 'Chinese whispers' effect does *not* occur. They want to ensure that the original message(s) passes unchanged along the chain from group to group. Most of all, they want to ensure that players at the end of the chain (teachers) will interpret Recommendation 2 in ways that are consistent with their original message. If this is true, it puts a whole new light on Recommendation 2. From being just one of 20 recommendations, it becomes the key for both understanding and implementing all the others. It stands to reason that if Recommendation 2 is aimed at those who have the final responsibility for implementing the essence of the full report, then the authors would choose the words of this recommendation very carefully. They would strive to ensure that there would be no ambiguity, no 'wiggle room' for teachers to misinterpret their intended message(s).

Let's look more closely at Recommendation 2.

> **Recommendation 2:**
>
> **The Committee recommends that teachers provide systematic, direct and explicit phonics instruction so that children master the essential alphabetic code-breaking skills required for foundational reading proficiency. Equally, that teachers provide an integrated approach to reading that supports the development of oral language, vocabulary, grammar, reading fluency, comprehension and the literacies of new technologies.**

What messages are embedded in Recommendation 2?

The wording of Recommendation 2 reflects its importance. It's lexically dense. It's chock-full of information. It's much more explicit than the other 19 recommendations. Furthermore, there are at least two kinds of message in Recommendation 2: *explicit* messages and *implicit* messages.

The explicit messages in Recommendation 2 are:

1. Teachers should teach phonics using a "*systematic, direct and explicit*" approach.
2. Somehow, they must ensure that this approach to phonics is part of an "*integrated approach to reading that supports the development of oral language, vocabulary, grammar, reading fluency, comprehension and the literacies of new technologies*".

The implicit messages in Recommendation 2 are:

1. Recoding print to sound ('decoding') is an essential prerequisite for constructing meaning from alphabetic script ("... *so that* children master the *essential* alphabetic code-breaking skills *required* for foundational reading proficiency").
2. These decoding processes have to be applied automatically (the children have to "*master*" these skills).
3. Automatic, mindless application can only be learned ("*mastered*") through intensive ("*systematic*"), teacher-controlled, ("*explicit*") lock-step, sequential ("*direct*") instruction.

Over the years, some of my research students have identified an important relationship between the explicit and implicit messages given to teachers engaged in professional learning. It is as follows:

> The ways they interpret (and subsequently implement) the explicit messages when engaged in professional learning depend on the degree to which they believe and/or accept the validity of the implicit messages underpinning them.
>
> *(based on Barton, 1992, 2000; Turbill, 1993; McKenzie, 2001; Bean, 2003)*

In my opinion, this places enormous professional responsibility on teachers. Should they accept at face value the implicit messages in Recommendation 2? What if there's some doubt about their accuracy and validity? What if the authors of the report have (unintentionally) overlooked or misinterpreted the data they've used to arrive at their recommendations? I suggest that we need to check the accuracy and validity of the implicit messages in Recommendation 2.

Implicit message #1: What's it all about?

The authors of the report claim that 'scientific, evidence-based research' conclusively shows that recoding print to sound (that is, 'decoding using phonics') is an 'essential prerequisite for constructing meaning from alphabetic script'. They base this claim on the findings of the US National Reading Panel's report, *Teaching Children to Read* (NICHD, 2000), describing it as "the largest and most influential investigation to date into the relative effectiveness of different approaches to the teaching of reading" (DEST, 2005: 31).

In the National Reading Panel report, this 'scientific, evidence-based research' is based mainly on the research of one of its panellists, Linda Ehri. Ehri (2004) claims that "research on word reading processes has distinguished several ways to read words". She goes on to argue that readers might identify a word from memory ("sight word reading"), or if encountering a word "never read before", could "transform graphemes into phonemes" and then "blend the phonemes" to form a word "with recognisable meaning". Or readers might use "analogy to known words" (Ehri, 2004, cited in McCardle & Chhabra, 2004).

It is important to understand that, in order to make such claims, Ehri (and those who cite her research) are forced to define 'effective' reading as *the ability to pronounce words in isolation*. It doesn't matter if the 'reader' doesn't comprehend the meaning of these words. As long as the words are pronounced accurately, those who make this claim argue that effective reading has occurred. In essence, this definition argues that once the automatic transformation from written to oral language has occurred (through accurate 'sounding out'), readers then convert these sounds to meaning by doing what they already do when constructing meaning after listening to spoken language – namely, by using the already established oral language process. This in turn implies that comprehension is not really an act of 'reading'; rather, it is an act of 'listening', and therefore part of an already established oral language facility. In other words, for advocates of this position, it is the automatic conversion from letter to sound that constitutes the act of 'reading'. Going from sound to meaning is made possible by pronouncing each word (aloud or as silent speech), which, according to this particular definition, allows the reader to 'hear' the word and retrieve its associated properties, including its meaning, from their mental lexicon. Once this is done (so the argument goes), meaning can be manipulated, along with the meanings of other pronounced words, in exactly the same way.

This view of reading can be represented thus:

Figure 1: A schematic representation based on Teaching Reading's *definition of 'effective reading'*

What kind of scientific evidence supports this view of reading?

In my opinion, there is no research that stands up to critical scrutiny. It is important to understand the implications that the view of reading in Figure 1 has on the research methodologies that its advocates employ to support their position. If one believes that the act of reading consists solely of the recoding of graphic symbols to corresponding sounds of oral language, then one will design, implement and evaluate intervention projects based on this view. One will also design research projects that measure reading ability based on this view. Thus, if one wants to prove that an approach to teaching reading that is based on implementing an intensive program of systematic, explicit phonics lifts reading ability, then one will use a pre-test of reading that comprises items based on the ability to make accurate letter–sound conversions, then implement a program that teaches the skills and knowledge necessary for accurate letter–sound conversion, and when the trial has finished, will administer a parallel version of the pre-test to measure growth. It all sounds very 'scientific'. The findings of such research have all the accoutrements of being 'evidence-based', and if the post-test scores rise significantly then surely this proves that the intervention has 'caused' reading to improve. What isn't made explicit is how those who engage in this kind of research actually define 'effective reading'.

This is the logic that underpins the US National Reading Panel's 2000 report into "scientifically based reading instruction". According to *The Australian* of 8 December 2005, it is also the logic that underpins the Australian report:

> ... the report – prepared by a panel of parents, teachers and academics led by Ken Rowe – has backed their push to embrace phonics as the key to reading. The inquiry calls for schools to embrace "systematic direct phonics instruction so children master the essential alphabetic code-breaking skills required for foundational reading proficiency".
>
> Australian Council for Educational Research chief executive Geoff Masters said yesterday it was clear a systematic approach was needed.
>
> "I think there's a very significant research base now in this area," Professor Masters said.
>
> *(Maiden, 2005)*

On the same day, the Federal Minister for Education's media release ran a very similar line:

> Today I have released the final report of the National Inquiry into the Teaching of Literacy. Entitled *Teaching Reading*, the report strongly recommends the use of a phonics-based teaching method – founded on proven and evidence-based strategies – to give students the best possible opportunity to learn to read and write in the early years of schooling.
>
> The report cautions against the exclusive use of the whole-language approach to the teaching of reading and finds it to be: "... not in the best interests of children, particularly those experiencing reading difficulties". (p. 12 of the report)
>
> *(Nelson, 2005)*

Should teachers uncritically accept these claims?

I don't think teachers should accept these claims, for two reasons. First, they're biased. Second, the claim that decoding to sound is an *essential* prerequisite for the construction of meaning flies in the face of very strong counter research-based evidence.

Let us deal with the claim of bias first. What's the basis for such a serious claim?

The bias in both the US and Australian reports

It is important to realise that the US National Reading Panel's reviewers selected and analysed a plethora of research studies carried out *only* by researchers who held the same view of reading as themselves. Alternative views, or research that supported alternative views, were not considered. In the years since its release, the US report has been thoroughly discredited because of this bias (see Coles, 2000, 2003; Krashen, 2001; Allington, 2002, 2004; Garan, 2002, 2005).

This bias is graphically described by Michael Pressley and Richard Allington (1999: 169) thus:

> As we reviewed the list of 2,500 NICHD-supported articles, we detected much less attention to the higher order processes related to comprehension than to the more atomistic components of reading, such as sound–letter and word skills. [...] It is easy to leave NICHD-driven discussions with the impression that sound-, letter- and word-level processes are all that really matters in reading, that if sound-, letter- and word-processes could be solved, literacy problems would be solved.

The Australian panel of analysts displayed exactly the same bias. They just weren't as blatant about it. They went through the motions of calling for submissions, and received more than 400 from a wide range of interested parties. They then used only those that supported their rationale and agenda to inform their recommendations, ignoring many submissions which offered 'evidence-based research' that conflicted with their view of effective reading. Of even greater concern is the fact that the most cited researcher in the references of both the *Teaching Reading* report and the *Literature Review* used as the basis of the report was Dr Ken Rowe, who was appointed to conduct the review. The ethical status of using so much of the research of the academic appointed to head the Inquiry to support the recommendations in the report is never raised. Another point of concern is that nowhere in the report is there an explicit declaration or qualifier that their definition of reading does *not* involve comprehension. Rather, it implies that their definition of reading (decoding to sound) is an already established scientific fact.

What about evidence-based research that does not support Recommendation 2?

There is a great deal of 'evidence-based research' which shows that for effective readers of alphabetic script it is *not* essential for them to decode the text to sound before they can access meaning (i.e. comprehend the text). This evidence shows two things very clearly:

1. That readers of alphabetic script *can* (indeed they *must*) access meaning directly from the visual display.
2. That the human brain has evolved to go directly to meaning without first going through sound.

One implication of this evidence is that teaching the full range of phonic generalisations *explicitly and systematically* before teaching comprehension strategies and skills is not only unnecessary, it could seriously work against developing lifelong, avid readers. In other words, it could be quite toxic for young learner-readers.

Let's consider some of the research that the writers of the report seemed to have ignored.

1. Prelinguistically deaf children

Prelinguistically deaf children are a naturally occurring control group. By definition, they can never proceed from print to sound, nor can they acquire phonemic awareness. Yet, as Helen Keller showed (and as teachers of profoundly deaf children continually demonstrate), humans with no possibility of ever having access to the sounds of language learn to read and comprehend complex meanings from written alphabetic texts.

2. The phenomenon of homonyms

Homonyms are words that are spelled differently but have the same pronunciation. The different visual shapes (i.e. different spellings) of words such as *rite* and *right*, *meat* and *meet*, *rain* and *rein*, *mince* and *mints* show that it is the visual shape, not the sounds, that determines meaning in these cases. This in turn indicates that alphabetic text can function 'logographically'. What this means is that two identical sets of sounds, such as "*The sun's rays meet*" and "*The sons raise meat*", can only be understood through the visual distinctions between *sun's–sons*, *rays–raise* and *meat–meet*. Sounding out these words will not make the meanings clear. This can only mean that there are lexical and grammatical features embedded in the visual display of alphabetic text that take precedence over sound.

3. The phenomenon of homographs

Homographs are words that are spelled the same but are pronounced differently. Here are some examples:

- The bandage was wound around the wound.
- The farm was used to produce produce.
- The dump was so full that it had to refuse more refuse.
- We must polish the Polish furniture.
- He could lead if he would get the lead out.
- Since there is no time like the present, he thought it was time to present the present.
- A bass was painted on the head of the bass drum.

These examples demonstrate that the spelling to sound system in English is governed *not* by an alphabetic, sound-based set of principles, but rather by the visual shape of the graphic display, supported by some grammatical and semantic background information. This is another example of the 'logographic principle' referred to above. Perhaps it is this principle which explains why readers of non-alphabetic writing systems such as Chinese can read complex-looking texts that are just as rich and complex in conceptual content as alphabetic scripts such as English.

In the examples above, the pronunciation of the words that have identical spellings (that is, they are visually identical) can only be determined *after* the reader has worked out what the sentence means. Trying to work out what each word 'sounds like' without first understanding what each 'means' in this context is an impossible task that would frustrate most learners. Given this, not only is it factually wrong to insist that speedy, automatic 'sounding out' of words is an essential prerequisite for learning to read, but it is also unethical to make the claims about the efficacy of teaching reading using a pedagogy based on the explicit and implicit messages in Recommendation 2.

4. Evidence from archaeology and evolutionary theory

Both archaeological and evolutionary evidence are also in conflict with the explicit and implicit messages in Recommendation 2. For example, recent evidence emerging from the fields of biological anthropology and neuro-anatomy show that:

- The human brain has evolved with both a visual and a phonetic path to meaning construction (Donald, 1991; Deacon, 1997);
- These paths are autonomous. One is not a prerequisite for the other, neither is one dependent or contingent on the other (Ramachandran, 2003);
- The brain's preferred route is to go from visual symbol, to meaning, then to sound (Donald, 1991; Deacon, 1997); and,
- In the use of cuneiform, hieroglyphic and other logographic scripts, direct grapheme to phoneme correspondence is impossible. Phonemes can only be known after the meaning of the symbol is understood. From a reading perspective, these systems have no more or no less expressive potential than alphabetic scripts (Strauss, 2005).

5. Evidence from psycholinguistic research and cognate fields

Numerous psycholinguistic research studies have been conducted over many decades. These continually and consistently demonstrate *that meaning must be accessed before sounds can be identified*. In the 1950s and 1960s, there was a plethora of rigorous, experimental research studies into speech perception, which disproved the hypothesis that the perception of continuous speech was merely one-to-one perception of individual speech sounds. A series of classic experiments by Miller, Heise and Lichten (1951), Miller and Isard (1963), Pollack and Pickett (1964), and Lieberman (1967) clearly demonstrated that there was *more to speech perception than the sounds that 'meet the ear'*. Lieberman (1967: 165) summarised the results of this research thus:

> Some of the distinctive features that specify each phonetic segment probably can be determined from the available acoustic signal. Other distinctive features cannot be uniquely identified. The listener therefore forms a hypothesis concerning

> the probable phonetic content of the message that is consistent with the known features. However, he [sic] cannot test this hypothesis for its syntactic and semantic consistency until he gets a fairly long segment of speech into his temporary processing space. The speech signal therefore remains unintelligible until the listener can successfully test a hypothesis. When the hypothesis is confirmed, the signal abruptly becomes intelligible.

According to Lieberman, this research shows that the sounds people hear are ultimately what they themselves have synthesised, and not what the speaker has produced. The reason why this speech seems clear to a listener is because it is self-generated. In this sense, what these research studies show is that the *clarity of speech is an illusion*. It is as if the listener fills in synthetically what isn't there and 'hears' the speech as perfectly normal, but through a distorting transmission line. Later research by Warren (1970), Warren and Warren (1970),Warren and Obusek (1971), Obusek and Warren (1973) confirmed this interpretation.

In similar vein, numerous studies carried out over several decades have also demonstrated that *there's more to reading for meaning than meets the eye*. These studies clearly show that reading for meaning does not presuppose a prior translation of print to sound. Rather, like the speech perception research of the 1960s, when engaged in the normal process of reading, readers (like listeners) form hypotheses of which words in the text are based on non-visual information and even ignore parts of the visual display. (See Weaver, 2002, for an extensive review of the research that confirms these claims.)

What about the other two implicit messages embedded in Recommendation 2? (See above.) I think it means that they can be ignored. If implicit message #1 is invalidated, then those that are dependent on it must also be invalid.

Does this mean that I'm suggesting that classroom teachers should abandon the teaching of phonics? The answer to this question is a loud and resounding series of "NO! NO! NO!" How is this possible given the evidence I've just presented? To answer this question, we have to ask the following question.

Does the alphabet (directly) support the act of reading alphabetic scripts?

The combination of English spelling, archaeological, evolutionary and psycholinguistic research evidence cited above strongly suggests that the alphabet did not evolve in order to help readers. *Rather, the evidence summarised above suggests that the alphabet evolved to support writing*. An alphabetic system such as English enables people to make marks on paper (and other surfaces) in a simple and consistent manner so that they will always *look the same*. In effect, alphabets are writers' 'tool kits' for putting words together. From a stock of just 26 basic shapes, all the words of the English language can be represented. Moreover, these 26 letters have names that define their shape. This means that novice writers can be told to write 'd', 'o', 'double l' (doll) instead of "First do a ball and put a stick on its right-hand side, then another ball, and then two sticks next to each other". This is a much more cost-effective way of constructing and transcribing meaning than logographic systems such as Chinese, ancient cuneiform or Egyptian hieroglyphics. In essence, the invention of the alphabet made writing and transcribing much easier for scribes, and the invention of paper and the printing press made the scribing process more accessible to more people. While this in turn made reading more accessible, it had little effect on the reading process.

While the alphabetic system gives the illusion that reading consists mainly of translating visual signs to their phonetic equivalents, there is strong archaeological and evolutionary evidence which argues that it does not, and the implications of assuming that it does need to be carefully considered. In fact, despite the repeated public claims around the *Teaching Reading* report that 'science' supports the centrality of phonics in reading, the arguments made by those who wrote it are based on a narrow, selective analysis of research studies that does not stand up to scientific scrutiny.

Given the financial and political pressure that the federal government can apply to the other target groups in the (metaphorical) 'Chinese whispers line' to ensure that each and every one of the report's 20 recommendations are enforced, what can classroom teachers, the players at the end of this (metaphorical) line, do? Can they implement Recommendation 2 in non-toxic ways and not be accused of subverting the intent of the report? I think they can. The table below explains how.

RECOMMENDATION	WILL BE TONIC IF ...	WILL BE TOXIC IF ...
2. "The Committee recommends that teachers provide systematic, direct and explicit phonics instruction so that children master the essential alphabetic code-breaking skills required for foundational reading proficiency. Equally, that teachers provide an integrated approach to reading that supports the development of oral language, vocabulary, grammar, reading fluency, comprehension and the literacies of new technologies."	i. *"Explicit, systematic, direct instruction in phonics"* is also *"mindful and contextualised instruction"*. ii. The alphabetic code is mastered *predominantly through student engagement in meaningful writing activities.* iii. An *"integrated approach to reading"* means teaching the skills and knowledge of effective reading as one of many ways of using symbols to construct and use meanings in the 21st century.	i. *"Explicit, systematic, direct instruction in phonics"* means teaching phonics using mindless, decontextualised repetitive, teacher-dominated drill and practice to match isolated fragments of oral language with alphabetic symbols. ii. The alphabetic code is taught predominantly through activities that emphasise *"recoding alphabetic symbols to sound"* (i.e. 'reading'), rather than vice-versa – *"writing the sounds of oral language using alphabetic symbols"* (i.e. 'writing').

Good luck. Remember to keep a straight face if the 'explicit, systematic phonics police' arrive at your school to see what you're doing.

References

Allington, Richard L. (2002) *Big Brother and the National Reading Curriculum: How ideology trumped evidence.* Portsmouth, NH: Heinemann.

Allington, Richard L. (2004) 'Setting the record straight'. *Educational Leadership*, March, 22–25.

Bean, W. (2003) 'The relationship between teacher learning and school culture'. Master of Education (Hons) thesis, University of Wollongong.

Barton, B. (1992) 'An evaluation of "teacher-as-co-researcher" as a methodology for staff development'. Unpublished Master of Education (Hons) thesis, University of Wollongong.

Barton, B. (2000) 'The relationships between mandated change, professional development and school growth'. Unpublished Doctor of Philosophy thesis, University of Wollongong.

Coles, G. (2000) *Misreading reading: The bad science that hurts children.* Portsmouth, NH: Heinemann.

Coles, G. (2003) *Reading the naked truth: Literacy, legislation, and lies.* Portsmouth, NH: Heinemann.

Deacon, T. W. (1997) *The symbolic species: The co-evolution of language and the brain.* New York: W. H. Norton.

Department of Education, Science and Training (DEST) (2005) *Teaching Reading: Report and Recommendations.* National Inquiry into the Teaching of Literacy. Canberra: Commonwealth of Australia. Accessed 30/3/06 at: <http://www.dest.gov.au/nitl/report.htm>

Donald, M. (1991) *Origins of the mind: Three stages in the evolution of culture and cognition.* Cambridge, MA: Harvard University Press.

Ehri, L. (2004) Teaching phonemic awareness and phonics. In P. McCardle & L. Chhabra (Eds), *The voice of evidence in reading research.* Baltimore: Brookes Publishing Company.

Garan, Elaine M. (2002) *Resisting reading mandates: How to triumph with the truth.* Portsmouth, NH: Heinemann.

Garan, Elaine M. (2005) 'Murder your darlings: A scientific response to the voice of evidence in reading research', *Phi Delta Kappan*, 86(6): 438–443.

Green, D. (2003) Children and print: Reading, In D. Green & R. Campbell (Eds), *Literacies and learners* (2nd ed.). Frenchs Forest, Sydney: Pearson.

Krashen, S. (2001) 'More smoke and mirrors: A critique of the National Reading Panel's Report on Fluency', *Phi Delta Kappan*, October, 119–123.

Lieberman, P. (1967) *Intonation, perception, and language.* Cambridge, MA: MIT Press.

McCardle. P., & Chhabra, L. (2004) (Eds), *The voice of evidence in reading research.* Baltimore: Brookes Publishing Company.

McKenzie, B. (2001) *Flowcharting: Its use as a tool for professional development.* Paper presented at the Australian Association for Research in Education (AARE) Conference, Fremantle, Western Australia, 2–6 December.

Maiden, S., (2005) 'Report backs literacy basics'. *The Australian*, 8 December.

Miller, G., & Isard, S. (1963) 'Some perceptual consequences of linguistic rules'. *Journal of Verbal Learning and Learning Behaviour*, Vol. 2: 217–228.

Miller, G. A., Heise, G., & Lichten, W. (1951) 'The intelligibility of speech as a function of the context of the test material'. *Journal of Experimental Psychology*, Vol. 41: 329–335.

Nelson, Dr Brendan (Minister for Education) (2005) Media release: *Report of the National Inquiry into the Teaching of Literacy*. Accessed 30/3/2006 at:
<http://www.dest.gov.au/Ministers/Media/Nelson/2005/12/n2061081205.asp>

NICHD (National Institute of Child Health & Human Development) (2000) *Report of the National Reading Panel: Teaching Children to Read*. Accessed 30/3/06 at:
<http://www.nichd.nih.gov/publications/nrp/smallbook.htm>

Obusek, C. J., & Warren, R. M. (1973) 'Relation of the verbal transformation and phonemic restoration effects'. *Cognitive Psychology*, Vol. 5: 97–107.

Pollack, I., & Pickett, J. M. (1964) 'Intelligibility of excerpts from fluent speech: Auditory vs. structural context'. *Journal of Verbal Learning and Learning Behaviour*, Vol. 3: 79–84.

Pressley, M., & Allington, R. (1999) 'What should reading instructional research be research of?' *Issues in Education: Contributions for Educational Psychology*, Vol. 5.

Ramachandran, V. S. (2003) *The artful brain, Lecture 3*. The Reith Lectures (The Emerging Mind), BBC Radio 4. Accessed 30/3/2006 at: <http://www.bbc.co.uk/radio4/reith2003/lecture3.shtml>

Strauss, Steven L. (2005) *The linguistics, neurology and politics of phonics: Silent 'E' speaks out*. New Jersey: Lawrence Erlbaum.

Turbill, J. (1993) 'From a personal theory to a grounded theory of staff development'. Unpublished Doctor of Philosophy thesis, University of Wollongong.

Warren, R. M. (1970) 'Perceptual restoration of missing speech sounds'. *Science*, Vol. 167: 392–393.

Warren, R. M., & Obusek, C. J. (1971) 'Speech perception and phonemic restoration'. *Perception and Psychophysics*, Vol. 9: 358–362.

Warren, R. M., & Warren, R. P. (1970) 'Auditory illusions and confusions'. *Scientific American*, No. 223: 30–36.

Weaver, C. (2002) *Reading process and practice: From socio-psycholinguistics to whole language* (2nd ed.). Portsmouth, NH: Heinemann.

Wikipedia: The Telephone Game. Accessed 30/3/06 at:
<http://en.wikipedia.org/wiki/Chinese_whispers>

A starting programme should be so designed that it provides for engagement of different children in different ways on different levels from the beginning.

(Clay, 1991:203)

4 Helping children learn to read

Jon Callow and Margery Hertzberg

Building on previous chapters, we explain how teachers scaffold children's reading development by exploring how important it is to understand the context of teaching reading, the many places that reading happens in classrooms, the various roles that readers take, and how different texts will teach readers different lessons.

How do children learn to read?

Space constraints dictate that only a brief account of learning to read can be provided here, and there are many useful books devoted to detailed analysis of what happens in this process (see, for example, Hill, 2006). As Cambourne illustrates in Chapter 3, there is a distinction between reading and decoding. Decoding is but one aspect of the process that enables a person to make meaning from text – that is, to read. We have found the following model (Harris et al., 2005) useful in explaining how important all the different aspects are in the reading process because it integrates the cueing systems with the roles of the reader. First, we briefly summarise the key features in this model and then, using two scenarios, highlight how these features are evident in classroom practice.

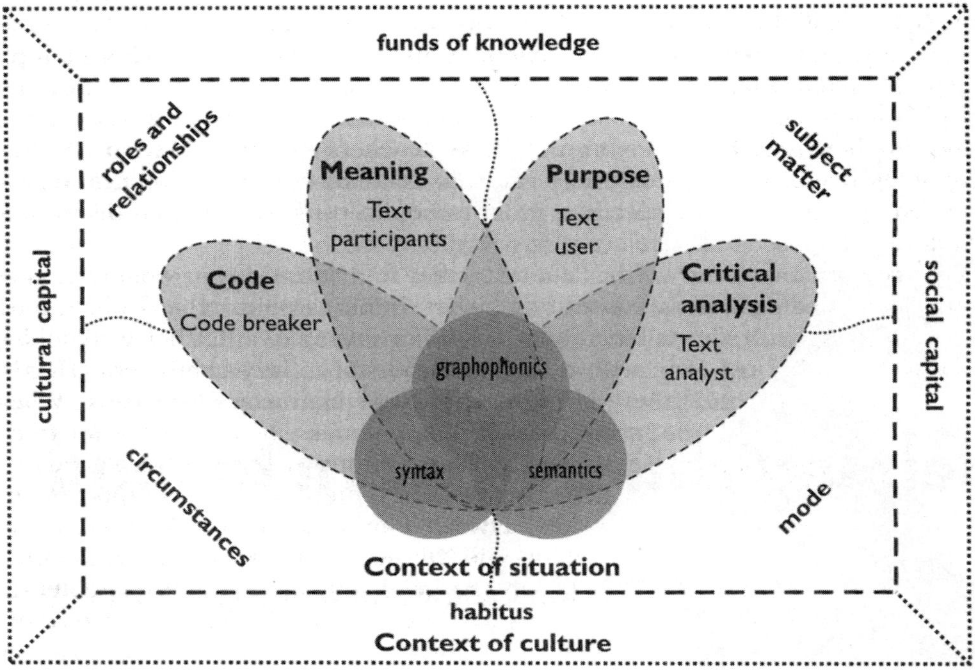

Figure 1: A model of reading as a set of social practices (Harris et al., 2005)

This model of reading provides a helpful visual representation of the reading process set within social contexts and practices. To gain meaning from a text, a reader uses a combination of cues: *semantics* (knowledge of the field), *syntax* (knowledge of grammar) and *graphophonic* (knowledge of the letter [grapho] and sound [phoneme]). All three cues (sometimes separated into four cues if the graphics are separated from the phonemic) are needed in order to read as opposed to decode. Based on the theory that all learning is socially constructed, Vygotsky (1975) and Luke and Freebody (1999) have shown how these cueing systems are inextricably linked to the cultural context, where readers have different types of cultural knowledge and social backgrounds (sometimes referred to as capital). They explain that the reading (making meaning) of a text is dependent on the text type, the background of both the writer and the reader, and the purpose of the text within any given cultural framework. Therefore, to be able to read a range of texts, a reader engages in all four roles (code-breaker, user, participant and analyst). Consequently, readers need to understand how a text relates to their background knowledge of the genre of the text, as well as their cultural knowledge and knowledge of the text's content itself, and what they are expected to do with the text as they read it. For example: "Am I meant to use a text about kites to find out how to make a kite or is it an imaginative story that I am to enjoy about a girl making a kite for a competition?" Furthermore, text analyst practices involve understanding that no text is neutral and how to appraise its effectiveness. Therefore, readers need to be able to consider critically the intent of the text – how the text aims to position the reader, and the message the text aims to convey.

Moreover, this model highlights that reading is a *process*, and illustrates how all aspects of this process are "interrelated and interdependent" (Freebody, 2004: 1). While just one or two aspects of the process might be emphasised within specific lesson time-slots, a balanced approach to literacy learning assumes that explicit instruction and learning activities in all aspects of the process occur within an overall program. It is also important to understand that reading is just one mode of literacy, and that learning to read happens within the context of the other modes (talking, listening, viewing and writing). Furthermore, literacy learning takes place in all subject areas. Excerpts from two teachers' classrooms have been selected to demonstrate these important principles.

Scenario One illustrates how early emergent and emergent readers engage with the various aspects we have noted above, while Scenario Two illustrates similar aspects but with an independent reader navigating in a hypertextual environment. We have examined both of these scenarios to draw out the reading theory that underpins the practices. Subsequent chapters provide more detailed examples of teaching and learning experiences based on these principles.

Scenario One

This inner-city Sydney Kindergarten/Reception classroom, early in 2006, had 20 children: 9 boys and 11 girls. Their ages ranged from 4 years and 7 months to 5 years and 6 months. All Australian citizens, they represented eight different cultural and linguistic heritages. The socioeconomic and educational status of their families also varied: shop assistants, professors, plumbers, and those seeking work. Seven of the children had been brought up in bilingual environments and could speak English, but at this stage their home language was stronger. Two children spoke only their home language but had minimal survival English skills. Eighteen children had attended preschool for at least one year – most attending the nearby preschool where bilingual education was encouraged and books were shared in the dominant language groups: Turkish, English, Korean and Mandarin. Reading ability ranged from early emergent to transitional, but the majority were early emergent.

The teacher, Sally, had met most children at Orientation Day the previous year, and parents had completed the school's questionnaire, developed to find out about home literacy practices and competencies. Sally's classroom was rich with a range of print media, and there were three computers. The book corner contained a variety of picture books and some short novels for the two students in the transitional stage. Some books were bilingual. For example, copies of *Peace at*

Last by Jill Murphy were in English, Vietnamese and Arabic. The dramatic play area had Australian newspapers in English, Chinese, Greek and Arabic scripts, and grocery items not only reflected a variety of cuisines, but also had labels on them in languages other than English. The front door had a welcome sign in nine different languages, and items in the room were labelled in both English and Mandarin.

In the first weeks, Sally planned to do a lot of shared and modelled reading with her class. The first book she selected was *Grandpa and Thomas* (Pamela Allen) and she had acquired 10 copies.

Session 1

Sally explained that they were going to read a story together and placed the book on the easel. She continued, "Our book today is called *Grandpa and Thomas* (pointing to the title). It is about a granddad and his grandson whose name is Thomas. Grandpa and Thomas are going to the beach ... Let's look at the front cover. What things are they taking with them to the beach?"

The children identified the various items, which Sally wrote on the whiteboard. The picture of a sandcastle was identified on the title page, and she revisited the notion that pictures on the title page often give the reader a clue as to what might happen in the book. Several students spontaneously and enthusiastically wanted to tell their stories about building sandcastles, so Sally asked if all the children had built sandcastles – they had. Children were then asked to share their experiences of building sandcastles with their "talking buddy". Following this 40-second unplanned discussion Sally, aware that the children were getting fidgety, began reading the book.

At its conclusion, Sally asked if anyone would like to make a comment about the book. Despina (with reference to the sandcastle getting washed away by the rising tide) responded that "we don't build sandcastles near the water because they get washed away". Many other children agreed. Sally returned to the relevant pages, and a class discussion followed. "See," said Joshua, "they've built it too close." Sally then asked talking buddies to speak about how best to build sandcastles (at which time she overheard Nicholas explaining how the moon influenced tidal patterns!). The following day, the children made 'playdough' sandcastles, which were displayed underneath a sign adapted from the text: "Swish, swash, swoosh sings the sea ... but don't come near me!"

Session 2

During group activities, Sally reread the book to a smaller group of early emergent readers. She wanted to concentrate specifically on some graphophonic aspects of the text. After a brief recap of the story, Sally read the first two pages and stopped after the refrain "Swish, swash, swoosh sings the sea". They talked about the words, and Sally explained that the author probably chose those words because they describe actions and sounds of the sea. The group then talked about waves and the actions they make. Returning to the pictures in the book, they established that at this beach the waves were gentle. Sally asked the children to imagine their arms were the waves, and they made the action of the waves while chanting "Swish, swash, swoosh". She then pointed to the first letter of each word in the refrain, and it was identified that, with the exception of 'the', the symbol was the letter 's'. Children were asked to think of other words that began with the sound /s/. Sally then pointed to the letter 's' in the final blend, explaining that when linked to the 'h' it has a different sound '*sh*' /ʃ/. Again, the children articulated the words with actions, with emphasis on the sounds /s/ and /sh/.

Sally then reread the book, and the children joined in the refrain each time – twelve times in all.

So what was happening here in terms of theories about teaching reading?

Reading context

By including the background of her children in such a scenario, Sally demonstrated several important principles:

- *Kindergarten is not the beginning of a child's reading development*
  Two children in Sally's class are in the transitional phase, and all the other children are early emergent and emergent. Although all children take part in the initial whole-class book-sharing session, explicit teaching of particular reading concepts is done in groups.

- *Reading is a universal practice*
  Sally acknowledges the linguistic backgrounds of her children and their parents. She includes a range of texts in various languages, and not just for social and emotionally inclusive reasons. Although reading instruction is in English, she wants the children to understand that reading is a message system (both conveyed and received), which happens in all languages.

- *Maintaining the home language aids English learning*
  Being bilingual is advantageous not only for social and emotional reasons, but also for cognitive ones (Cummins, 2000; Krashen & McField, 2005). The school can only afford to offer support for the Mandarin speakers (the dominant minority language group), but Sally affirms the importance of maintaining the home language (oral and written) to all parents because development in literacy practices, irrespective of the language, helps children develop in terms of the *process*. To this end, both the school and the municipal library stock a variety of bilingual texts, and parents are encouraged to read with their children in the home language. However, as English is the dominant language, and she believes that oral language is important in the development of reading, Sally structures her lessons to maximise opportunities for all children to talk – hence the 'talking buddies' strategy. For more ideas about this, see Dufficy (2005).

Resources for teaching reading

There are many valuable resources that can be used. Here we look at the variety of reasons why Sally is using this specific book early in the first year of primary school with this class.

Selecting the resource

Although it was not available in big book format, Sally selected *Grandpa and Thomas* for shared/modelled and modelled/guided reading because the book catered for the varied literacy abilities in her class, and she planned to integrate events in this book in other curriculum areas, including Mathematics. The font was large enough for 20 children, and she had 10 copies for individual use in smaller group time.

Choice of subject matter

Grandpa and Thomas is culturally and linguistically appropriate because every child frequented nearby beaches, enabling existing field knowledge in terms of content and vocabulary to be drawn on. While some did not know the English term 'spade', they knew how to build sandcastles using one, and so the task was simplified. They were "learning a new label for old learning" (Gibbons, 1991: 6), and so their practices as *text participants* were less problematic.

The language and genre of the book

Although independent reading of the written text was not achievable for this group, the language in this well-crafted narrative picture book aided the children in a number of ways, such as through its use of repetition and predictable grammatical structures. Other features of this text are:

- *A familiar genre*
  The narrative picture book genre was familiar from previous literacy experiences, both at home and at preschool, and so familiarity as *text users* made it quicker and easier for the class to understand the story. They knew the prediction strategy of using the pictures as clues, and they were working with a good example of a story that is told in part only from reading the pictures. Therefore, the book lent itself to a lot of oral work, another feature of good literature.
- *An authentic literary text*
  It is beyond the scope of this chapter to detail why well-written literature is usually a better resource to use than many commercial basal reading schemes (Meek, 1988), but, as Gibbons states, "while overall language development supports reading, so too does reading support language development. Language is learned through reading; it is not simply a prerequisite for it." (Gibbons, 1991: 97).

The orientation on the first two pages of *Grandpa and Thomas* illustrates this well:

> Grandpa and Thomas go to the beach.
>
> Thomas carries his bucket and spade.
>
> Grandpa carries his bag, the big picnic rug, and the green umbrella.
>
> Thomas spreads out the big picnic rug.
>
> Grandpa puts up the green umbrella.

The repetitious nature of both phrases and words is good for early emergent readers in terms of *code-breaking* practices. At the same time, it is authentic and meaningful text. For instance, rather than "puts out the big picnic rug", Allen uses the more semantically correct term "spreads". In this way, children not only have access to real language, they have access to new language learning.

Teaching the reading process with younger readers

This first scenario snapshots some of the roles being practised during the shared/modelled reading of a book with a whole class, followed by a guided/modelled reading session for early emergent students.

Session 1

Text participant practices are emphasised in the 'Before reading' section to activate prior knowledge about both the genre and its content. As discussed previously, language development aids reading development. The 'talking buddies' strategy (especially important for EAL learners and for those with speech processing difficulties) enables all children to use the language functions of, for instance, 'explanation', 'description' and 'opinion'. By explaining the activity (and introducing the subject), Sally attends to a crucial teaching principle called *focusing* (Swain, 1995). From this position, children can then predict possible content words and events. In the 'After reading' section, a mixture of *text user* and *text analyst* practices are evident when children respond to the open-ended question. For example, Despina's disapproval about the sandcastle being built so close to the high tide mark demonstrates critical appraisal. Using this unexpected response, because it engaged so many children, Sally included an activity that involved making sandcastles with a caption that innovated the refrain in the text. This not only validated their opinions, but also attended to rhythm and rhyme (phonemic awareness).

Session 2

As Cambourne explains in Chapter 3, the phonological skills needed for learning to write and learning to read are different. Sally's primary focus in this scenario was on *code-breaking* reading practices, but she also integrated her handwriting lessons by focusing on 'b', 'g', 't' and 's' to help children understand the relationship between the written symbol (grapheme) and its varying sounds (phonemes) in authentic texts. In this session, Sally concentrated on the grapheme 's' and its corresponding phonemes /s/ and /sh/ in the refrain "Swish, swash, swoosh sings the sea". In addition, /s/ is the beginning phoneme for many other words such as *spade, slip, slop, sunscreen, sand, stone* and *sandwich*. Chanting the refrain with actions was fun and helped engage the children, but at the same time attended to Sally's purpose of hearing the sounds in words using both gesture and vocalisation (Hertzberg, in press).

In our next scenario, we'll see how older readers involved in different types of reading activities, drawing on different resources, use the same text reading practices to gain meaning.

Scenario Two – for older readers

Sue's Year 5 students were studying countries of the world as part of their social studies theme. The students were from a mostly middle-class area, with a variety of cultural and linguistic heritages. While most were independent readers who read and enjoyed a variety of literary texts, Sue understood the importance of developing their sophistication and depth of reading, as well as exposing them to a range of texts and information sources.

As the class learnt about various countries, the students' reading and writing skills were called upon, enabling them to locate relevant information, skim and scan for key ideas using books, and then understand what they were reading, as they prepared to take notes for their own writing and PowerPoint presentations. However, as the literacy demands of the topic became apparent, Sue became aware that her students needed to learn how to read websites and multimedia texts in a way that was different from reading print-based or narrative text (Callow & Zammit, 2002).

Sue began to guide her students as they read electronic texts together. Onto the screen unfolded a selection of words, images, menu bars, captions, frames and sponsored advertisements – not the norm for a science textbook. Both Sue and her students learned that reading 'on screen' is quite different from reading a book.

Guided reading as a text analyst

One important focus for learning to read websites was the source of information. Was the information reliable? Who was providing the information? In order to help students read more critically, a selection of questions was used as a prompt during their guided reading of the screen. Some of these included:

- What is the address of the site?
- Who is the provider of the information? Can you identify a known organisation or institution?
- Is the institution regarded as credible?
- What are the qualifications and position of the provider?
- Is it associated with a commercial institution or business, which may have a financial benefit in representing certain kinds of information and perspectives but not others?

The use of keywords when searching for information using a search engine helped students understand that using different search terms can produce quite different results (**text user**). One group searched Yahoo.com using two different search terms: i.) 'Papua New Guinea' and ii.) 'Papua New Guinea AND culture'. The students worked in pairs in their small group, and then compared the results that the search engine supplied. For example, entering the first phrase provided more general sites, including educational, government and business sites. The second term yielded more specific sites, and therefore was often more useful for their particular purpose.

Some students accidentally went to Yahoo.com.au and came up with different search results, which prompted discussion of what the 'au' suffix means when using a website. This also complemented the first activity.

Guided viewing

A further activity focused on the visual reading of the screen. Again, some key questions helped the groups begin to read aspects such as layout, colour and overall quality of the page. These included:

- What is the general care and quality of the design, organisation, and presentation of the material?
- Does it look as if it were put together by people with attention to detail?
- Is there too much flash and gimmickry on the page, and does this connote a certain lack of seriousness?
- Is there a date of the 'last update'?
- What is the purpose of the page?
- Who is the audience for the page? Would it appeal to this audience? Why?
- How do you navigate within the page – by internal links/headings or do you have to scroll down?
- What is the general organisation of the page? How are images, navigation icons and text placed on the page?

These Year 5 students, who were mostly independent readers with print-based text, were learning new lessons from these electronic texts. Even those who were confident using computers and the web needed scaffolding around the more complex reading roles that these new types of texts offer. Now let's explore some aspects of this scenario.

Teaching the reading process with older readers

The idea that learning to read somehow stops when students can read books independently is challenged in this classroom. While we know that learning to probe more deeply into novels and literary texts, to learn about aspects such as themes, symbolism and figurative language, should be part of an upper primary classroom, in this classroom the teacher also spent guided reading time helping students to become more critical and competent readers of electronic texts. Many of the students would no doubt be very competent in accessing and clicking around a website, but the skills for understanding the purpose, effectiveness and reliability of websites are not those that just happen – they require explanation and discussion with a skilled mentor (Leu et al., 2004).

It's also worth noting that the beauty of guided reading, with any type of text, is that it scaffolds the reader to focus on a particular skill or concept and then lets them explore and practise the skill in a small, controlled context. After this, they are encouraged to go off and independently apply their new skills in other contexts and activities (Hornsby, 2000). These types of reading lessons are always tailored to meet the needs of the learners, as well as the demands of the text they encounter. For some, the skill will be quickly and easily learnt, while others will need to revisit it a few times, practising with a partner or the teacher.

If we consider the different roles that readers undertake when reading a screen or website, it becomes clear that some reading lessons learnt from books will transfer quite easily, while others will need to be approached differently. Consider these two paragraphs from different websites about Papua New Guinea:

> Papua New Guinea is a raw land, remarkably untamed and as variegated as swamp and jagged limestone; mud and moss forest; suffocating heat and Highland chill; plumed, pearl-shelled villagers and prosaic hill people; tiny tree kangaroos and enormous Queen Alexandra Birdwing butterflies.
>
> *(www.lonelyplanet.com)*

> Papua New Guinea is the largest developing country in the South Pacific region. Its 463,000 square kilometres of land area, a sea area of 3.12 million square kilometres and 600 separate islands make up one of the most diverse repositories of geographic, biological, linguistic and cultural wealth on earth.
>
> *(AusAID www.ausaid.gov.au)*

Reading this with a whole class on a video projector or overhead, or with a small group on a computer screen, Sue might focus on the various roles that a reader might take on. Both paragraphs have quite challenging new vocabulary – *variegated, prosaic, repositories, linguistic*. Here, the code-breaker role would come into play, drawing on phonological knowledge to pronounce the words, as well as working out their semantic meanings, using contextual and morphological clues (*variegated* comes from the words 'vary' and 'variety'). Sue might also make a link to grammar and spelling, where adjectives such as *geographic* or *biological* come from the nouns *geography* and *biology*. Also, the etymology of prefixes such as *geo-* and *bio-* go back to Greek origins.

Having made meaning of each paragraph, Sue might then ask her students: "What text is presenting more factual-sounding information? What text might be trying to persuade you?" Here, she is teaching her students to take on not just a *text participant* role, by reading about New Guinea, but she is moving on to include the *text user* and *text analyst* role: What do I do with this information? What points of view are being presented? As teachers and literacy educators, we would want to argue that the teaching of reading needs to include these critical roles at pertinent points (Knobel & Healy, 1998).

While the points above could easily be done with a printed text, the fact that this is a website means we should consider the multimodal and hyperlink elements, which will change how we read this text. Let's look at the other elements on the screen.

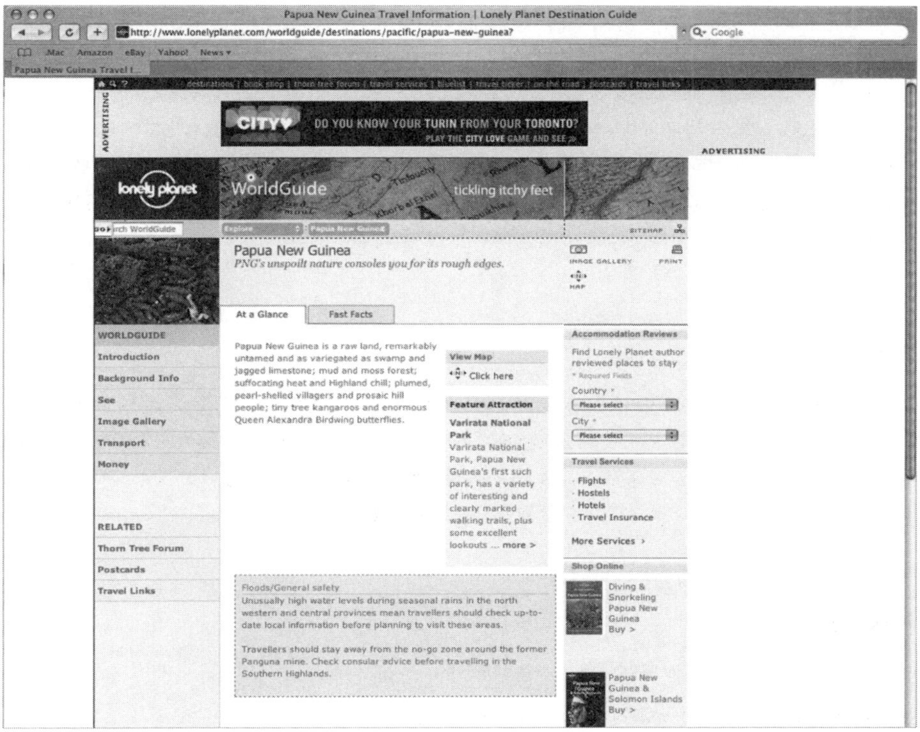

(Source: http://www.lonelyplanet.com/worldguide/destinations/pacific/papua-new-guinea/)

Reading the screen itself involves interpreting the visual images, using the side menu bar, clicking on image galleries or on a map, and selecting related links. While many students will confidently explore and click through, there are some important skills and concepts here for teachers to introduce to their learners, particularly in relation to how the written text relates to the other links and options on the screen. Hence, Sue's reading lessons have a multimodal focus, bringing different issues to students' understanding of literacy.

In a guided reading session, a 'think aloud' might be a really useful strategy to draw students' attention to cues about the page. A teacher might say to the group as they view this page: "Well, when I read that first paragraph, I thought that the language was very descriptive and quite exciting. But when I looked at the other things on the screen, I noticed that there were accommodation reviews, travel service links and an online shop. Straightaway I began to think that this website is probably trying to sell me something, like a holiday or a book, so it's using language to make me *want* to go there, to persuade me. If I'm looking for factual information, I'll need to be careful to make sure it's accurate and correct."

So we can see that the act of reading in an online context still involves the cue systems and roles of the reader and, just as with print-based texts, these need to be taught and explained to students (Zammit & Downes, 2002). However, most published information books don't offer package holidays or online shopping, so skimming and scanning a print text seemingly offers fewer diversionary options. While these types of interactive, hyperlinked experiences are all part of reading for students in the 21st century, the reading theory that we have outlined for our younger readers using print-based narratives still applies to older, independent readers using multimodal, electronic texts.

Conclusion

In this chapter we have shown just how complex learning to read really is. So, too, is teaching reading! We not only need to program to ensure that all roles are interdependent, we also need to consider learning to read as one part of the literacy jigsaw that cannot be taught in isolation from talking, listening, writing and viewing.

References

Allen, P. (2003) *Grandpa and Thomas.* Australia: Penguin Books.

AusAid Country Programs Papua New Guinea web page. Accessed 30/3/06 at: <http://www.ausaid.gov.au/country/png/png_intro.cfm>

Callow, J., & Zammit, K. (2002) Visual literacy: From picture books to electronic texts. In M. Monteith (Ed.), *Teaching primary literacy with ICT.* Buckingham: Open University Press.

Clay, M. (1991) *Becoming literate: The construction of inner control.* Portsmouth, NH: Heinemann.

Cummins, J. (2000) *Language, power and pedagogy: Bilingual children in the crossfire.* Clevedon, UK: Multilingual Matters.

Dufficy, P. (2005) *Designing learning for diverse classrooms.* Sydney: Primary English Teaching Association.

Freebody, P. (2004) Hindsight and foresight: Putting the four roles model of reading to work in the daily business of teaching. In A. Healy and E. Honan (Eds.). *Text next. New resources for literacy learning.* Sydney: Primary English Teaching Association.

Gibbons, P. (1991) *Learning to learn in a second language.* Sydney: Primary English Teaching Association.

Harris, P., Turbill, J., Fitzsimmons, P., & McKenzie, B. (2005) *Reading in the primary school years* (2nd ed.). Melbourne: Thomson.

Hertzberg, M. [in press] Dramatically 'e'NGAGED. In Fair Go Team, *School is for me: Pathways to student engagement.* Sydney: Priority Schools Program, NSW Department of Education and Training.

Hill, S. (2005) *Developing early literacy: Assessment and teaching.* Armadale, Victoria: Eleanor Curtain Publishing.

Hornsby, D. (2000) *A closer look at guided reading.* Armadale, Victoria: Eleanor Curtain Publishing.

Knobel, M., & Healy, A. (1998) *Critical literacies in the primary classroom.* Sydney: Primary English Teaching Association.

Krashen, S., & McField, G. (2005) 'What works? Reviewing the latest evidence on bilingual education'. *Language Learner*, 1(2): 7–10, 34.

Leu, D. J., Jr., Kinzer, C. K., Coiro, J., & Cammack, D. W. (2004) Toward a theory of new literacies emerging from the Internet and other information and communication technologies. In R. B. Ruddell & N. Unrau (Eds), *Theoretical models and processes of reading* (5th ed., pp. 1570–1613). Newark: International Reading Association.

Lonely Planet – Papua New Guinea web page. Accessed 30/3/06 at: <http://www.lonelyplanet.com/worldguide/destinations/pacific/papua-new-guinea/>

Luke, A., & Freebody, P. (1999) 'A map of possible practices: Further notes on the four resources model'. *Practically Primary*, 4(2). Accessed 30/3/06 at: <http://www.alea.edu.au/freebody.htm>

Meek, M. (1988) *How texts teach what readers learn.* Stroud, UK: Thimble Press.

Swain, M. (1995) Three functions of output in second language learning. In G. Cook & B. Seidlhofer (Eds). *Principle and practice in applied linguistics: Studies in honour of H. G. Widdowson.* Oxford, UK: Oxford University Press, pp. 125–144.

Vygotsky, L. (1976) *Thought and language.* Cambridge, MA: MIT Press.

Zammit, Z., & Downes, T. (2002) 'New learning environments and the multiliterate individual: A framework for educators'. *Australian Journal of Language and Literacy*, 25(2): 24–36.

Acknowledgements

We warmly thank Valerie Martin, Sue-Ellen Rosenberg, and the children in KR for their assistance, and Katina Zammit for her classroom research examples.

Controversy about the 'best' way to teach reading cannot be resolved by prescribing a single method. Because there is no clearly documented best way to teach beginning reading, educators who are familiar with a wide range of methodologies and who are closest to children must be the ones to make decisions about what instructional methods to use.

(International Reading Association, 1999)

5 Achieving a balanced reading program in the early years of schooling

Robyn Wild, with
Clive McArthur and Kim Self

Introduction

Throughout our lives, as we observe and interact with people, we are learning about our world. As we grow, we're constantly watching, trying to do things for ourselves, and being helped and supported by others. This support can take many forms, some more helpful than others.

In our role as teachers, we need to offer our students the most effective support possible. As Callow and Hertzberg demonstrated in Chapter 4, we need to explicitly model and demonstrate information that will support our students as they become readers and writers. But what do we need to demonstrate, and how do we know it's what our students need at that particular time? Closely observing our students to find out exactly what they *can* do will assist us to find answers to this question. We need to compare this assessment information with pathways of development as outlined in syllabus documents. To supplement this information, it's essential that we build ties with children's families and communities, and share information with them. This sharing of information is also necessary with support staff. Ongoing observation and assessment of students gives us our starting point. Activities that link children's lives with integrated learning across subject areas help make learning in schools real and relevant.

But once we've gathered this knowledge, as well as made teaching and learning decisions based on our assessment, we need to ensure that our teaching is systematic, well planned and thoughtful. Our explanations need to be clear and should offer students explicit information that will best support their learning. We need to organise our classrooms and programs so that we can strengthen each child's learning.

So how can we best do this?

Modelled reading

Teachers model reading constantly: when they refer to their wristwatches, when they read messages, when they access information from computer screens, when they check their diaries or read SMS messages. In each case, they are demonstrating that reading is infused throughout their everyday lives and across many social situations and contexts.

Modelled reading also occurs when teachers read aloud to the whole class. During modelled reading, teachers read to and for students, and it is the teacher who chooses the text. Students can hear the language of literature, can be transported into different worlds, experience adventures and see how others solve problems. They can hear factual texts, poetry, novels and picture books. Sometimes the text is chosen for sheer enjoyment and is often linked to the class unit of work. Modelled reading, or *reading to children*, can happen at any time during the day, not just within the literacy session. Texts used while reading to students are usually *not enlarged*, even though they are being read to the whole class.

Shared reading

While demonstrations are extremely powerful, teachers will find that they need to do more than just read to and for their students. They regularly need to be more explicit – and using enlarged texts with the whole class or small groups will help them to do this. While reading texts that students can *see* and *read together*, teachers can invite students to join in with the reading in a non-threatening way. Teachers can focus on specific aspects of the text and on how information may be drawn from it. For example, the teacher's purpose may be to highlight a particular reading strategy, spelling or grammar generalisation, or to focus on phonological information, specific vocabulary, text structure, comprehension or critical thinking skills. Their choice is dependent on student assessment and their teaching purpose. Teachers need to be explicit during each shared reading/enlarged text session. They need to make the purpose of each shared reading session clear to students, and suggest ways that this information may be transferred to students' reading of other texts.

Shared reading does not involve multiple small copies of the same text – it requires teachers and students to read one (usually enlarged) text together. These texts could be written on the board, on a chart, in a big book, or on an overhead, data projector, enlarged computer screen or smart board – just so long as all the students can see the text.

By reading each text several times, teachers can refocus students' attention towards different aspects of the text. Students who would be hesitant or unable to access the text independently, or who come from non-English speaking backgrounds, are better able to actively participate with and gain meaning from the text when it's read together in this way.

Independent reading

Students need to read independently and silently for sustained periods every day. It is during this time that they practise their new-found reading skills, explore a range of texts, and begin to discover the magic of literature and the wealth of knowledge that can be found in factual texts. They need to be given the opportunity to choose what they read and to share their findings with others.

Teachers need to provide a wide array of texts and to ensure that routines are in place that enable sustained, silent reading time daily. They need to model reading for pleasure as well as reading for information. While observing students reading independently, teachers can assess students' attitudes to reading and their engagement with books.

Guided reading

> Guided reading, because it is a bridge to independence, is perhaps the most important component in the mix of teaching and learning activities in a literacy program.
>
> *(Ministry of Education, 2002)*

Guided reading allows teachers to cater for the different reading abilities of students in their classes. Students of similar abilities are grouped together and are offered support so that they may read texts successfully by themselves. Teachers choose texts that students have not seen before and that will challenge them in some way. The challenge for students may be in decoding the text, in gaining meaning from or in thinking critically about the text.

Teachers need to know their students' strengths as readers, and should support and challenge them as they access more demanding texts. Students need to make a link between what they know about reading familiar texts and how they can best use this information to gain meaning from unfamiliar or slightly more difficult texts.

Grouping students for guided reading is dependent on teacher judgement. Teachers will form groups based on their assessment of children's reading abilities and the strategies that they use as they access texts. Grouping students in particular ways may be appropriate for only short periods, as each child's developmental pathway will be unique and dynamic.

Teachers should choose guided reading texts with care. These texts must have enough familiar components to ensure that students may best solve each new reading challenge by themselves.

It is the teacher's role to support and guide readers through this process.

The guided reading process

The teacher and a group of students sit facing each other. The new text is introduced through focused discussion where the teacher may, for example, introduce new vocabulary or make text-to-text and text-to-life connections. Students will be given their own copy of the text. The teacher will have access to a whiteboard or easel.

The teacher sets a purpose for the reading by, for example, asking students to search for specific information in the text or to focus on a particular reading strategy. Each student reads their own text silently and independently. (Asking students to read in a whisper may be an appropriate transition for young students as they learn to read silently.) The teacher highlights specific aspects of the text and the language it contains on the whiteboard during the discussion that follows the reading. Assessment information may be gathered while the teacher observes students as they read and discuss the text. This process may be repeated as students read and discuss additional sections of the text within the one guided reading session.

To conclude the guided reading session and to make the teaching and learning points explicit to students, the teacher should revisit the purpose of the reading and summarise what's been learnt. Afterwards, students can reread the text independently and may complete literacy activities around the text.

Literacy activities

To enable teachers to work with small groups during guided reading, students may be asked to read independently or to complete activities that require them to explore texts, to reinforce strategies and to practise reading. These literacy activities may be linked to the classroom topic, reinforce understandings introduced during shared reading, relate specifically to guided reading texts or focus on specific reading skills and strategies.

Table 1: Overview of suggested literacy activities

Literacy activities may include:	
reading centres	• independent reading for pleasure, to search for information or to complete a task • reading with a friend • reading text around the wall • reading a story to/with a buddy • oral reading onto tapes
writing centres	• using clipboards to copy text from the wall • using clipboards to search for specific words or letters that are on display around the walls • independent and collaborative writing for different purposes (e.g. lists, letters, greeting cards, recipes etc.) • writing on the computer • innovating on a text
oral language centres	• communicative activities, e.g. barrier games (often used by ESL teachers) • storybook retellings, using puppets or other prompts • listening to taped stories • collaborative sequencing of known stories using pictures • retelling known stories to a partner or onto a tape • acting out a story or play or readers' theatre
sentence centres	• copy sentences from enlarged or independent reading texts onto strips of paper and match them with text • order sentence strips, adding the correct punctuation • order sentences on an overhead projector

word centres	• create a word wall of high-frequency words • copy words from the word wall onto paper or by using magnetic letters or rubber stamps • create flashcards from known big books and match them to the text • sort flashcards into patterns (e.g. based on initial letter or letter pattern) • arrange words on flashcards in alphabetical order • play memory games using flashcards • write or make high-frequency words on individual chalkboards, whiteboards, with plasticine, with letter tiles • search for high-frequency words in texts • identify rhyming words • match word cards with pictures or objects • use the overhead projector and plastic letters to display high-frequency words
letter centres	• form letters using plasticine, string and glue, paste and sand, pipe cleaners etc. • match upper- and lower-case letters • match plastic letters to high-frequency word cards • put letters in alphabetical order • sort letters by shape (i.e. tall letters, letters with tails) • match magnetic letters to the appropriate pages in alphabet books • search for words with specific letters or letter pattern in magazines, newspapers or independent reading texts

(Adapted from NSW Department of School Education, 1997; Jackson Blakemore & Weston Ramirez, 1999; Ministry of Education, 2002.)

Writing

Skills and understandings learnt while reading influence our writing. Conversely, our writing experiences will affect our reading (Brown & Cambourne, 1989). Therefore, it is essential that we consider supporting students as writers, as they learn to read. While there is not sufficient space to discuss writing in detail, suffice to say that we should design modelled, shared, guided and independent writing experiences that focus on the writing process and the text types, as well as skills (such as grammar, spelling and handwriting). The examples that follow later in this chapter demonstrate how reading and writing, talking, listening and viewing are all interrelated.

Assessment

Ongoing assessment is essential if teachers are to gain deep knowledge of students in their classes, and this is discussed in detail in Chapter 7. Teachers need to ensure that they observe students while they work independently and collaboratively throughout the day. They also need to gain specific information about how each student reads. The taking of running records (also described in Chapter 7) provides teachers with specific diagnostic information, as well as ensuring that students are reading texts at their instructional level. Running records should be taken regularly, and more often for those students who are causing concern. Running records help teachers identify which of the three cueing systems students are overusing or underutilising. Analysing the miscues, as well as asking students to discuss or retell the text, will help identify how well students understand what they're reading.

Analysing running records will also show teachers that the texts they've chosen for particular groups of students are matched to their reading ability and are therefore appropriate to use with them during guided reading sessions.

Organising the literacy session

How can we fit modelled, shared, guided and independent reading and writing opportunities into each literacy session and also have time to closely observe students as they work? Even though there is no one definitive organisational pattern that will fit every teacher and every classroom situation, what follows is a suggestion. It enables teachers to closely work with students, as well as to observe them, as they participate actively in reading and writing tasks independently or collaboratively or in small groups with the teacher.

The boxes below indicate class groupings. Boxes that stretch across the entire page indicate that teachers will be working with the whole class. Boxes on the right-hand side indicate that students will be working independently, i.e. without the direct assistance of the teacher. Boxes on the left-hand side indicate that teachers are working with individual students or small groups.

A focused reading session

Teacher works with whole class during shared reading session, using enlarged texts. 10–15 minutes	

Teacher works with individuals (to take running records) or with small groups (for guided reading sessions). 10–15 minutes/group	Students work individually or collaboratively as they read independently and complete literacy activities. 30–40 minutes

Teacher reads to the whole class during modelled reading session, using picture books, novels etc. 10 minutes	

Teacher works with whole class during shared writing/joint construction, creating enlarged texts together. 10–15 minutes	

Teacher works with individuals or with small groups (for guided writing sessions). 10–15 minutes/group	Students work independently or collaboratively as they write. 30–40 minutes

(Source: NSW Department of School Education, 1999. For a more comprehensive weekly literacy planning overview see NSW Department of School Education, *Teaching Spelling K-6*, 1998, pp 106-108.)

Specific focuses on skills development (e.g. grammar, spelling, etc.) will take place within the shared, guided and independent sessions, within the context of real texts.

Two teachers, Clive and Kim, now describe how they organise their balanced literacy sessions.

Case Study 1: Kindergarten in a suburban school, *Clive McArthur*

I am in my third year of teaching after working in the corporate world for 16 years. I teach a Kindergarten class in a suburban Sydney school. The school has a largely Anglo population and has a strong sense of community. There are 22 children in the class, in ages ranging from 4.5 to 5.5 years. It is a split site, with around 150 children at the K–2 school and another 150 children at the 3–6 school, which is approximately 1 km away. Most of the children have experienced a lot of literacy in both preschool and in their homes. There are three children who require ESL support and one who attends external speech therapy sessions.

It is such a challenge to develop, implement and maintain a balanced literacy program, but what a wonderful challenge. Literacy is perhaps the most important thing we teach. Without the skills of reading, writing, viewing, talking and listening, it is much harder for students to achieve success in the other Key Learning Areas (KLAs). In short, every day is a reading and writing day. So this is how it looks in practice in my Kindergarten classroom.

The first weeks are spent in helping the children to adjust to their new environment and to feel comfortable in trying out new things. This is the time when I observe the children and assess what they can and cannot do. Some don't know the names or sounds of any letters, nor have much grasp of the format of text, while others have had extensive exposure to literacy in the home environment and are already reading and writing. As there is extensive contact with Kindergarten parents, it helps to discuss this with them. Assessment includes observing fine-motor skills (how they use scissors and hold a pencil), and things like their knowledge of letter names and sounds, as well as each child's general interests. My aim is to develop a productive learning environment for each individual.

Talking and listening is developed in helping them to interact effectively (by discussing and modelling the skills) and in weekly news where each student speaks in front of the class, after practising at home. Weekly topics relating to the current themes are set at the start of each term. For example, this week we are focusing on our favourite story. Last week we talked about our pets or a pet we would like to have.

Organising the classroom is an important priority. After watching the students in individual and group activities in the first week, they are seated in small groups of four to six with peers with whom it is expected they will be productive and happy. There is a large open area at the front, with minimal clutter on the front board and wall, a construction area, dress-up area, reading area (stocked with a regularly changed variety of books on display), and a maths, puzzles and craft area. Routines of knowing where to find things and knowing what they will be doing on a particular day and time help productivity enormously.

There is a lot of explicit modelling of reading and writing right from the beginning of the school year as I do everyday things in the classroom. I introduce phonics in the first few weeks. This is integrated with weekly themes and includes a shared reading session with a 'big book' reread each day of the week. The students become progressively familiar with the text as the week progresses. I use a variety of literary and factual texts for this shared reading time. We discuss how the book relates to them, as well as the technical aspects of the text including grammar and genre. Independent reading is also encouraged from day 1. Students are given silent time after recess or lunch to select and read independently. These books are often also used in impromptu shared reading sessions throughout the day.

By Term 2, students are taking home a book, tailored to their appropriate level, to read with their mum or dad every night. The parents are advised how to best help their children develop their skill and enjoyment of text. Students progress through the levels of home readers, receiving certificates for each homework card of completed books. Along with the home reading routine, parents are invited to participate in individual shared reading sessions at school every day. Each student spends a few minutes with an adult each afternoon revisiting their 'home reader' from the previous day. In this way, they have a chance to go over the same material with a different set of helping eyes and ears to assist in their development. Also, well-informed parents help by advising me of students who they feel are ready to progress to another level.

Parents are also involved in the technology program. I have four computers in my room. Once a week the children are given individual guidance. They become familiar with common computer icons, the keyboard and the use of the mouse using Word and KidPix. They love this time, and it becomes another frame of reference to discuss the variety of formats in which we use the written word.

Guided reading sessions (see earlier comments) begin around Term 2. The children are separated into groups according to their reading level. Twice a week, each group sits in a circle with me, and we read a book together. In this way, they learn from each other at the level in which they are developing, and I get a regular opportunity to observe the progress of each individual. Some students progress more rapidly than others, and these sessions enable me to move them up or down to more appropriate levels as needed. This program can only be implemented when the other students are capable of working independently on other activities while I spend time with each successive group. Sometimes this is supported by the ESL teacher.

With many of the reading activities, there is a linked writing activity. Each week an individual letter of the alphabet is thoroughly explored using songs, the big book, and through games, poems, writing activities and creative arts. Handwriting is practised in a variety of ways. At the start of the year the children are given an alphabet chart, which they personalise by colouring it. The chart is then laminated, along with their name in large foundation script. It is one of the first things they put on their table each day. Another part of the daily routine – which ensures fairness (of paramount importance to a 5 year old) in allocating who gets to do 'special things' during the school day – is a list of all students' names arranged alphabetically, which is placed prominently on the front board. We refer to this constantly during the day. Students quickly become familiar with their peers' names. Learning to write their own name through labelling their work is an important step in their writing development.

Each student has their own story-writing book. They use this in developing a growing awareness of the many purposes for using spoken and written texts. They write diary entries, stories, descriptions, narratives and lists. They build banks of written words along various themes (e.g. home or games), and banks of rhyming words that enable many students to enlarge their written vocabulary quite quickly.

Outcomes for each activity are listed in my weekly program so that I can see clearly from the outset that I am covering what I need to in the syllabus. It is important to teach to these rather than to a unit of work so that I can be clear about what I'm doing at any moment in the classroom. In general, I expect that by the year's end most children will know the names and sounds of the letters of the alphabet, will have an appreciation of the format of text (e.g. upper- and lower-case letters, full stops, question marks and exclamation marks), will be able to appreciate that text has different uses and purposes and – most importantly – will enjoy literature. If they can leave Kindergarten with an attitude of excitement toward talking and listening, reading and writing, then it has been a great year.

Case Study 2: Year 1/2 in an inner-city school, *Kim Self*

I have just moved schools and am now Assistant Principal at an inner-west Sydney school. In some ways, I am starting all over again.

Setting up for literacy, and especially reading, for a new class is a multifaceted task that changes from year to year. Each class brings with it its own complexities and needs that must be taken into consideration. I usually begin the year with a focused literacy theme that provides many opportunities for modelled and shared reading and discussion about texts, language and the strategies we use to read and view text. This gives me information on the students and their understanding of and abilities in reading. This theme links reading, writing, talking and listening, and other KLAs.

At the same time I am reviewing assessment data from the previous year and conducting my own assessment to ascertain what the students can do and where they need to go next. Developing routines and setting up structures is an essential focus of the first few weeks. This process may take longer in some circumstances, depending upon individual classes and schools. Setting up the environment, physical and behavioural, for an effective balance between instruction and productive, meaningful and targeted practice is an essential step.

Also essential for optimising student learning and engagement is the use of systematic and explicit shared and guided teaching. Knowing exactly what students need can only be achieved through ongoing assessment. (See Chapter 7 for more details on assessment.) Much of a teacher's assessment is on the spot and observational. I use an assessment sheet (see page 66) for each guided reading group, which prompts me in areas I am targeting and allows me to easily and quickly record observations for later reflection. I find this helps me build a clear picture of each child and gives me excellent information that I may otherwise not recall from memory.

My literacy session begins with shared reading. The text is large enough for students to see and may be a big book or an enlarged photocopy. I endeavour to use a variety of real texts such as maps, brochures, advertisements, timetables, and so on. The text is chosen to fit in with a unit or theme we are covering and links very closely with my writing focus. This means that the grammatical features I select to focus on in shared reading are the same as those I would focus on in guided writing. Guided writing could be the joint construction of a concept map, diagram, description of character in a narrative text, and so on.

This session allows me to explore how texts work, the structures and features (e.g. labels, visual literacy features, grammatical aspects), and/or how readers successfully gain information from texts using all four roles of the reader: decoder, participant, analyst and user (Luke & Freebody, 1999). I feel it is important to expose students to texts that promote discussion and critical thinking. It is the teacher's questioning that facilitates students' higher-order thinking. This may mean that the text being studied is above their level as a decoder, but it allows them to discuss texts at a higher level. This is especially important for students who struggle to decode. They need opportunities to access and discuss more complex written language and themes that they otherwise would not be exposed to. There may be a difference in their ability to discuss a text and read a text. They need opportunities to develop the metalanguage necessary to develop concepts and understanding. Their reading ability is not always indicative of their ability to talk about texts and understand text structure. These students are often reluctant to contribute in whole-class shared reading, but are less intimidated in a small group situation.

Guided reading

Level: Mid-Stage 1

Group: ____________

Term:	1	2	3	4

Week:	1	2	3	4	5	6	7	8	9	10	11

Learning To:

- ☐ Uses pictures to predict content
- ☐ Uses meaning when reading – predicts text on what they've read so far – does it make sense?
- ☐ Uses visual cues to read word – does it look right?
- ☐ Attempts to use analogy to read some new words
- ☐ Uses structural cues – does it sound right?
- ☐ Makes an attempt to decode unfamiliar words
- ☐ Monitors errors and rereads to self-correct
- ☐ Reads in a phrased and fluent way
- ☐ Chunks words to decode using fingers
- ☐ Reads attending to word endings (e.g. 'ing', 'ed')
- ☐ Identifies a sentence in text

Learning About:

- ☐ Can orally summarise or retell a text with teacher prompting
- ☐ Answers questions about the text
- ☐ Can talk about simple visuals and their purpose, e.g. illustrations, glossary, contents
- ☐ Can identify different text types/purpose
- ☐ Can discuss different parts of the text
- ☐ Can identify action verbs, nouns and adjectives in texts and talks about purpose
- ☐ Talks about simple punctuation and purpose
- ☐ Talks about purpose/ audience of real texts

Information Skills:

- ☐ Title
- ☐ Author
- ☐ Illustrator
- ☐ Text types
- ☐ Purpose/audience
- ☐ Speech marks
- ☐ Capitals
- ☐ Contractions
- ☐ Logos
- ☐ Symbols

Group notes:

Name: ____________

Name: ____________

Students then move onto reading activities. These may be based on the shared reading, the texts they are reading at their instructional level, tasks linked to the mechanics of reading (e.g. word recognition), or reading using familiar or easy texts to practise strategies independently.

While this is occurring, I withdraw groups for guided reading. These groups are flexible and responsive to student progress and development. As students plateau or make gains, I regroup them to meet their learning needs. Ideally, my groups are no larger than six, and the lowest achieving group is limited to no more than four. I try to see the neediest students each day. During this time I like to begin with a quick introductory activity (e.g. 'Elconian boxes' – letter boxes for each sound in a one-syllable word) or a sight word game, using magnetic letters to make words. I then ask students to read a familiar text. I always keep copies of previous texts available so that students can practise their reading strategies with confidence on known texts. Before commencing reading, I always prompt students to use strategies they need to become automatic in.

I see my developing readers for at least three guided reading sessions a week. They are consolidating skills and are moving onto higher level decoding skills such as chunking. I see my role as guiding them and building bridges to help them read more fluently and efficiently. It is my role to prompt them to become independent and confident in the skills of reading texts so that they are focused on making meaning from them. The ability to be able to chunk words is an important step in reading. I have a cue chart on the wall that I refer to at the beginning of each guided session to remind them to use their finger to chunk words or to focus their eyes on word endings until they can do it more automatically. I ask them to read a section of the text with certain questions to answer, and we discuss where the answer was located in the text. I try to ask questions that require them to use captions, titles, and visual literacy, and to connect information between sentences. We discuss words they may not know and how to work out what they might mean. We also discuss any comprehension work they are completing independently, as I feel it is important to teach students how to read questions successfully.

I see my more competent readers for two guided reading lessons per week. They may be looking at the same text or they may be looking at a selection of texts based on a theme such as 'fables' or 'weather'. I will focus on certain aspects of the text and ask guiding questions (developing the four roles of the reader) for them to reflect on or answer when exploring the text they are reading. I encourage students to use reciprocal teaching to develop them as active learners. I believe it is important that engaged reading is central to the reading session. This means that my students will read several new texts a week until they are able to read chapter books.

Conclusion

It's not the modelled, shared, guided or independent tasks in themselves that make the difference to students' literacy learning – it's what teachers *do* during these sessions that's important. It's when teachers are focused kid-watchers, and have a sound theoretical understanding of how students learn to read and write, that they can offer the most appropriate support to each of them.

References

Brown, H., & Cambourne, B. (1990) Evaluation in the whole language classroom: A collaborative research project. In E. Daly (Ed.), *Monitoring children's language development*. Carlton South: Australian Reading Association.

International Reading Association (IRA) (1999) *Using multiple methods of beginning reading instruction: A position statement of the International Reading Association*. Newark, Delaware: IRA. Accessed 18/4/06 at: <www.reading.org/resources/issues/positions_multiple_methods.html>

Jackson Blakemore, C., & Weston Ramirez, B. (1999) *Literacy centres for the early years classroom*. Sydney: Pearson/Longman.

Luke, A., & Freebody, P. (1999) 'A map of possible practices: Further notes on the four resources model'. *Practically Primary*, 4(2). Accessed 30/3/2006 at: <http://www.alea.edu.au/freebody.htm>

Ministry of Education (2002) *Guided reading Years 1–4*. Wellington: Learning Media.

Ministry of Education (2003) *Effective literacy practice in Years 1 to 4*. Wellington: Learning Media.

NSW Department of School Education (1997) *Teaching reading in Early Stage 1*. Sydney: Curriculum Support Directorate.

NSW Department of School Education (1999) *Teaching reading in a multi-age classroom*. Sydney: Curriculum Support Directorate.

NSW Department of School Education (1998) *Teaching Spelling K-6*. Sydney: Curriculum Support Directorate.

The meeting of minds is a problem that faces all teachers with all children. However, the problem is particularly significant in schools serving communities with cultural and language identities different from those of the majority culture... Their communities include indigenous groups, long-term 'involuntary minorities' (Ogbu, 1991), and recent immigrant groups (McNaughton, 2002)... without a deliberate teaching focus for these children and their families, classrooms will continue to be risky places for them.

(McNaughton, op.cit.: 18)

6 Meeting diverse reading needs in a multilingual classroom

Sue Bremner and Paul Dufficy

Introduction

Australia is one of the world's most culturally and linguistically diverse countries. Multilingual classrooms, where a number of children from different primary language backgrounds are learning English as an additional language (EAL), are a feature of most urban centres and some regional areas in Australia. Figures for 2001 show that 40% of Australians are migrants or the children of migrants, while approximately 25% of our current population were born overseas. More than half this number were born overseas in countries where English was not the language of state and public participation. In all, people from 200 countries now live in Australia (Federal Race Discrimination Commissioner, 2001). To take just one state as an example, government schools in New South Wales enrolled 191,818 students for whom English was not their primary language in the 2002 school year. This figure represented 25% of all government school enrolments, compared with 19.8% in 1996 (New South Wales Department of Education and Training, 2002).

Not unexpectedly, these children and young people come from a wide range of backgrounds and often have very different educational experiences. As a consequence, they also have quite distinct language and learning needs. For example, some will have been born in Australia, while others will have arrived quite recently as temporary or permanent migrants. Some recent arrivals will be refugees. For children not born in Australia, prior educational experience may cover a wide spectrum – from little, or severely disrupted, schooling to a six-day schooling week often accompanied by additional coaching. Initial English proficiency will vary as well. If children born in Australia already have brothers and sisters at school, then in all likelihood they will enter Kindergarten with some English. First-born children, on the other hand, may not. Depending on prior experience, some recent arrivals may have already begun to learn English in their country of origin. Along the same lines, some recent arrivals will be literate in their primary language, while others will learn to read for the first time in English. Among those lucky enough to have learnt to read and write in their primary language there will be differences as well. For example, like English, some languages use an alphabetic script (Thai, French), while others do not (Chinese); some use the Roman alphabet (Spanish, Vietnamese), while others do not (Thai, Korean); some use punctuation quite similar to English (Indonesian), while others use no punctuation at all (Thai); some languages are written left to right like English (Thai), while others are written right to left (Arabic); and, unlike English, some languages use additional symbols to indicate tones (Vietnamese).

It is important to take this diversity into account when planning our literacy program, but we must also remember that, past a certain stage, the specific literacy needs of EAL children will need to be met while we are teaching the whole class. For this reason, narrow, single-method solutions, or unbalanced emphasis on one particular approach, will most likely fail to assist all children in our classrooms to read and comprehend proficiently. Of course, there is money to be made in such blinkered approaches, and it is not uncommon for there to be strong links between so-called 'scientific' research, bureaucrats and publishing houses to justify a single-method focus (Garan, 2002).

The next part of the chapter will address aspects of reading that may benefit EAL students who are learning to read in English.

Foundation elements

For EAL children, one of the most essential elements for initial success in learning to read, and for later, more sophisticated engagement with written texts, is ongoing oral language development in English. It is, first, the bedrock upon which all other approaches rest, and then later provides a tool to be able to critically talk about texts. With conscious teacher guidance, an ongoing oral language focus can play a pivotal role in vocabulary development (Weizman & Snow, 2001), and when used as an exploratory and speculative tool, heightens syntactic (word order) awareness. It can also be used to emphasise the reading–writing connection, which is vital for a student engaging with the alphabetic principles of English.

Children who use English as their primary language will have had about five years of exposure to spoken English prior to the beginning of formal schooling. Most syllabuses, which are written for English speakers, presuppose this exposure to oral language, and rightly so. However, this lag in exposure to oral language is significant, and it needs to be constantly addressed in order for our bilingual children to be truly successful readers.

The second foundational element of a successful reading program for diverse, multilingual classrooms is a lot of reading. Readers who are read to by teachers come to see reading as an enjoyable, social practice. And children who read a lot get better at reading. Now, as simple as this sounds, bulk reading in practice is sometimes harder to engineer. Well-stocked libraries help; setting aside time for in-class individual reading is appropriate; gathering a wide range of written texts to support a unit of work is important, especially examples of the kind of text you might want the children to write; and reading to the class everyday – from big books to novels to poems to the newspaper – is essential.

The third foundational element is the development of a classroom ethos where children and young people are assisted to come to see that books and other written texts are important parts of their lives – both in and out of school – and that engaged reading has its own intrinsic rewards beyond test scores. As has been said, at the heart of engaged reading is the notion that "participation is a key to proficiency" (Guthrie, 2004: 4).

Playing with sound – phonological processing strategies

Reading in English involves recognising the sounds that are depicted by the letters on the page. 'Phonological awareness' is the overarching term we use to refer to a consciousness of the sounds and sound patterns that we later refer to in writing. There are a number of strategies that we can use to help develop children's phonological awareness.

Playing with oral onomatopoeia helps students hear the sounds and manipulate them in choral reading, chants and other low-stress situations. A fun place to start is with common animal sounds – for example, Australian dogs may *bow-wow*, and American dogs might say their own name (*Ralph!*), but Vietnamese dogs go *ciou ciou ciou!* Many stories for young children have wonderful examples of oral onomatopoeia, such as John Burningham's Mr Gumpy books, Nette Hilton's *A Proper Little Lady*, and a host of fables, folktales and nursery rhymes. Of course, EAL children most likely will not have experienced the literary canon of, say, *Mother Goose*, and so it is important for teachers to check out any assumed familiarity.

Having the rhymes available for students to refer to is of great benefit, particularly when the text is supported by graphics (e.g. *Hickory, Dickory, Dock*). Promotional material (remember the *Slip, slop, slap* campaign?) and media texts can also be used.

'Phonemic awareness' is part of phonological awareness, along with rhyme awareness, sound discrimination, sentence segmentation and word segmentation. Rhymes support the reading process because students need to hear and tune in to the sounds that words end with. The initial sound is the *onset*, and the final part of one-syllable words is the *rime*. It is the rime that rhymes. Rhyme is closely related to analogy, which is a strategy that beginning readers use to decode new words. They link the new word to a word they are already familiar with: e.g. *cats, rats, mats; tail, rail*. Of course, not all rhyming words look the same, and so that is another teaching point: *there, hair, mare* all sound the same, but they do not look the same at all. Another useful thing to keep in mind is that onomatopoeic words sound like their meaning (e.g. *bang, slippery, flop*), but most words that sound the same, through rhyming, have little to do with each other in terms of the semantics, or meaning. With rhyme, you are emphasising the sounds that the letters make.

EAL learners often tune in to the beginning sound of a word, and miss the end. Many final letters in words are hardly enunciated at all, particularly the final 'r' – and the Australian accent can make it even more challenging to tune in to the end. Not surprisingly, with reading, EAL learners also just read the beginning letter, look at the length of the word, and then make a reasonable guess. When focusing on the end of a word, it is important to support students with picture clues so they get a context for when they are likely to come across the word. The 'look' of a word helps – for example, knowing the look of *sees, seas* and *seizure* will help when making sense of the meanings of *oversees, overseas* and *seizure* (Wallace, 1988).

A further strategy is the use of alliterative sentences, made up by the children, to focus on the beginning sounds, such as variations of alphabet books (e.g. Graeme Base's *Animalia*); or make up alliterative sentences to go with pictures (e.g. *Anno's Animals* by Mitsumasa Anno). There is a vast array of suitable books on the market. Ask students to bring in their favourites from their local library.

Sometimes the students just fade out when they say words because they are not sure how to say the end of the word. Again, choral readings and chants give them a chance to play with language in situations that are not threatening. Chants, where the readers have to change intonation and volume, are also good because the exaggeration helps the students hear the sounds. For example:

FIVE little monkeys, jumping on the BED,

one fell down and bumped his head. (*high-pitched voice*)

Momma called the doctor and the doc-tor said (*deep, stern voice*)

NO MORE MONKEYS JUMPING ON THE BED!

One, two, three, four, FIVE (*EAL children often say "fi" for "five"*)

Once I caught a fish alive

Six, seven, eight, nine, ten

Then I let him go a-gain.

Mirror, mirror, on the wall (*in everyday usage, the -or at the end of mirror is muted*)

Who is the fairest one of all?

Young readers need to understand that letters are constant (an 'r' is always the letter 'r'), but sounds change (*There are three birds over there*). Consonants may sound different depending on their placement in a word, and also on the placement of the word in a sentence. An EAL learner may not hear the sound because it is not emphasised. If they do not hear it, they certainly will not spell it. The reading–spelling connection is well documented (for example, Bean, 2000). Activities that help readers follow along with the text are useful. These include following a taped story, or a shared reading where they can follow along with the text. This gives students a chance to see the words, and hear the words as they are used, and to hear another voice besides the teacher's.

Vocabulary learning

All children begin school with between five and six thousand words of their primary language. For some Kindergarten children, these words might be Arabic, or Spanish, or Urdu, while for others they will be English. The dual task for EAL children is to both catch up and keep up because, as they begin to learn English words, the English-speaking children are continuing to expand their vocabulary. As daunting as this may seem, there are two things that EAL children have going for them. First, they learn the everyday words of English reasonably quickly (in about two years), and about 80% of most written texts are made up of the most common 2000 words in English. And second, while EAL children may initially be behind in quantity, they are capable of learning words that are new to all children in the class, at the same rate.

As children move through primary school, however, they increasingly encounter new vocabulary that is not of the everyday kind. This is the specialised vocabulary of maths, science and the humanities, and it will remain a mystery unless it is taught specifically.

The key, therefore, is to place a much stronger emphasis on vocabulary teaching than is often the case. If the extent of vocabulary teaching runs to the weekly spelling list, definitions from the dictionary, and a find-a-word, then few benefit.

For all children, new words will be learnt best when the following principles guide our practice:

- The context of use for the new word is made clear. This means that the new word is connected in some way to what the children already know.
- There is ample opportunity to think deeply about the new word. This means that we provide activities that challenge children to think about the new word from different angles and perspectives.
- New words should be recycled frequently. This means that children should meet and reuse the new word in a variety of purposeful activities.
- We demonstrate daily our own fascination with words. This means that we share our curiosity about the origins of words, that we share with the children examples of words we might have seen used in different ways outside the classroom, and it also means being playful with language.

Space does not allow a full account of the many different kinds of activities that assist vocabulary development; however, with these principles in mind, the following is a broad activity domain to creatively develop the word knowledge of all the children in our classes.

Linking words

One of the key factors in knowing a word – apart from its dictionary definition, how to spell it, and how and when to say it – is knowing the company it keeps. Put another way, we need to help children make links between words. There are a number of ways of doing this, including *clines*, *clusters*, *synonym cloze* and *topic overviews*, examples of which can be found in a recent PETA publication (Dufficy, 2005). Further examples include *word walls*, *exclusion brainstorming*, *contextual redefinition* and *semantic feature analysis*, which are all described by Carrasquillo et al. (2004). Related to a semantic feature analysis, one further example is a *collocation grid*.

A collocation grid typically takes a number of nouns, say, from a chapter of a novel or a factual text, and places them across a horizontal grid. The vertical grid might contain adjectives. The following grid (Activity 1) was given to children after they had read a report about venomous snakes.

Activity 1

Do this task with a partner. Some of the words definitely go together, some might go together, and some do not go together. If you think the words definitely go together, use a tick [✓]. If you are not sure, use a question mark [?]. If you are sure they don't go together, use a cross [x]. I have done one for you as an example. We will discuss our thinking when everybody is finished.

	animal	reptile	snake	body	eye	skin	tail	fang	scale
an enormous									
a sharp									
a harmless	✓	✓	✓	X	X	X	?	X	X
a smooth									
a venomous									

The important point here is that the children are encouraged to think about words and how they may or may not be connected to other words. Bringing specialised words to consciousness, linking them to known words, and recycling them through various purposeful activities will give momentum to children's reading. If this process is underpinned by a collaborative, participative orientation, then the spin-off benefit is that oral language is constantly being developed as well, which, in turn, feeds back to the processes and activities, becoming a spiral of literate development.

Fluency

Giving children in multilingual classrooms opportunities to develop their reading fluency is important because fluency frees up "processing space" (Center, 2005: 164) for comprehension. Here, again, space limits the range of tasks that might be used to encourage the development of fluency, but the following all relate to the reading of a text more than once in order to promote fluency for all readers.

Repeated readings

The first example of repeated readings[1] is where the teacher places a short text (about four to five sentences at most) on an overhead projector. The whole class reads the text

[1] Pauline Gibbons (2002: 94) calls this example of repeated readings a "vanishing cloze".

together. The teacher asks a child to select a word, and this word is rubbed out. The whole class reads the text again, *including* the omitted word. Another word is chosen, rubbed out, and the class reads the whole text again. The process is repeated until there are no words remaining. The result is that the children now know the text off-by-heart. While a bit of a party trick, it means that less fluent readers can now join in, say, a sentence sequencing task with great confidence as they are not bound to a letter-by-letter approach to the text. Knowing a text (or other things for that matter) off-by-heart might seem a little old fashioned, but young children often know their favourite books from cover to cover, and many in the past learnt to read from the religious texts they had memorised.

Another version of repeated readings is to give children a text that is reasonably familiar to them and is also related to something being worked on in class, and ask them to read it several times, with greater fluency as a goal. It might be appropriate at times to ask the children to time themselves to see if they can get faster each time.

The next version of repeated readings is slightly different as it includes listening. In the following example, the goal was for the children in a multilingual Year 3/4 class to read the following teacher-written text.

A historical recount of the journey of the First Fleet

The First Fleet left Portsmouth in England on 13th May 1787. At first the weather was fine, and the fleet reached an island called Tenerife off the coast of Africa on the 3rd of June. The fleet remained in Tenerife for a week and took on supplies of fresh meat, fruit and vegetables. The weather was now very hot, and so conditions on board the ships became very harsh.

After leaving Tenerife the fleet sailed south and reached Rio de Janeiro on the 5th of August. The fleet stayed here for almost a month, and once again fresh supplies were taken on board.

The fleet now began the crossing of the South Atlantic Ocean. The weather was terrible, and many of the convicts and crew suffered from seasickness. At last, on October 13th, the fleet arrived at Table Bay at the Cape of Good Hope. The fleet stayed at Table Bay for about a month, and again took on fresh supplies as well as horses, cattle, sheep, goats and chickens.

The fleet left the Cape of Good Hope in November and sailed across the Indian Ocean. The fleet sailed around the bottom of Van Diemen's Land, and the ships arrived in Gamay on the 18th January 1788. Six days later, on the 26th of January, the fleet dropped anchor in Warrane.

To start, the teacher showed the class a short video excerpt of an 18th century sailing ship and speculated a little with the class about the conditions on board such a ship. Next, explaining that they were going to read about the journey of the First Fleet, the teacher put a world map on the overhead projector that indicated only the starting point (Portsmouth) and the destination (Warrane/Port Jackson). Taking turns, volunteers came up and, with an overhead pen, drew what they thought was the likely journey of the fleet. Apart from one student, Erdem, who set sail across France, most got to Warrane/Port Jackson with a few stops along the way. The teacher then played a tape of the historical recount. Once completed, the teacher rubbed off the earlier route predictions and labelled the map in more detail, including the oceans and ports mentioned in the recount. Next, the children were given identical maps (already labelled) and drew the route as they listened a second time. The class then listened a third time, as the teacher mapped the route on the overhead map.

At this point the class began discussing aspects of the journey and puzzling over some questions raised by the teacher. In time, the children were paired up and returned to their desks where they received an envelope with the recount cut into four sections. Their task was to sequence the sections to complete the recount.

Once done, the children then might complete a three-level guide (Dufficy, 2005: 139), research some of the questions raised previously, look for some vocabulary exploration, or use the text to practise reading fluently. Having the text on tape is useful because less able readers can listen to the text and read along. It is important, when thinking about fluency activities, that we use texts that are not too difficult to read, are relevant to what the children are learning about, and that we take the load off students, where appropriate, by strong contextual support, by prior listening and, where possible, by having the text on tape.

Reading for meaning

The sorts of activities that we assign our children give strong messages to them concerning what counts as reading. Some students will be successful decoders but will be unable to reflect on what they just read. Many of the comprehension passages that come with commercially produced reading materials do emphasise literal readings, and do not have much in the way of students defending or justifying their choices and selections.

Rather than use this sort of material as it is presented, consider making the activities more interactive. This gives students a chance to say aloud what they have read, and to use 'book language' aloud in a low-stress, but accountable, situation.

Have students work in pairs, with one question sheet between them. Students are expected to discuss and agree on an answer before they record it. They are also expected to locate the evidence from the text to defend their choice. When the answers are discussed as a whole class, students all have to indicate how they got their answer. This is particularly useful for inferential questions, as the information is not directly retrievable.

Reading activities that have proved to be successful tend to highlight meaning and the language features that help students gain access to the meaning. These include, but are not restricted to, the following examples in Table 1.

Table 1: Some successful reading activities

Activity	Examples	Emphasis
Sequencing a text they have had read to them	Text reconstruction of a story or a particular type of text with a salient structure. Use physical manipulation first, with cut-up sentence strips. Later, students can use numbers to order the text.	Students could track how the plot develops, following characters and/or events, or use clues such as conjunctions and adverbs of time for a linear narrative or a biography.
Turning prose into graphics	A story map in English or a timeline of real events in other areas of the curriculum.	The words that 'move the events along', such as dates, temporal connectives and other cohesive devices can be pointed out to readers.
Answering specific questions, and justifying their responses using the text's information	Question sheets can be used that ask 'who', 'what', 'where', 'when', 'why' questions, so long as the process of responding is interactive.	Justifying responses and indicating where the clues for the responses were located.
Extensive reading (reading widely for specific purposes)	This includes scanning material for specific information, skimming to get the overall gist, and covering a quantity of material without close, intensive reading (Hedge, 2003).	This helps students read quickly, looking for key words or phrases, as well as formatting clues, to find information they may later read more closely.
Matching the main ideas of a paragraph with the paragraph	This can be done as a matching exercise, using lines of physical manipulation, or the summaries could be distributed to pairs of students. As the extended prose is read out, students have to listen to see if they have the matching main ideas.	This is one way of modelling how to pick out the main idea from a read passage. Summarising is a sophisticated, powerful reading strategy that needs to be explicitly taught.
Reading excerpts from text that focus on generic structure (the overall 'unfolding' of the text)	This could be a story with a twist, or a well-written factual report, discussion or argument. Students need experience with texts to help them with prediction of the structure of texts.	This is a good way to familiarise students with text construction, and paragraph construction, as the end of paragraphs foreshadow or preview what is to follow.
Readers' theatre	Students take part in readers' theatre, rehearsing a small part initially, and then taking on other roles. Students rehearse in small groups before presenting to the class.	The repeated readings, with students taking on different roles, along with the voice manipulation required for taking on different characters, supports building up their fluency and reading for meaning, as they learn to read with appropriate expression.
Word/picture matching activities	Students match pictures with what they are hearing, then reading.	This might involve matching a picture to a description.

Communicative cloze	Students work in pairs to read a familiar passage, and either guess the missing words together, or one partner has the missing words and supplies clues as to the meaning.	This is useful for synonyms and shades of meaning, if non-neutral words are removed (such as *considered, yelled, horrible*), and for technical vocabulary if topic words are removed (such as *nocturnal, pouch, joey*).

EAL learners likely will rely on schooling as their main model of literate, book language – the language they will probably have to use in their written work, as they express their own ideas and opinions. Students need a range of models to give them exposure to both literate language and the more conscious instructional interactions with how to read texts. By models, we mean models of the texts themselves, models of how to read the different types of texts ('reading strategies') and actual human beings – other readers.

References

Bean, W. (2000) PEN 124: *Ways to teach spelling*. Sydney: Primary English Teaching Association.

Center, Y. (2005) *Beginning reading*. Crows Nest, NSW: Allen & Unwin.

Carrasquillo, A., Kucer, S., & Abrams, R. (2004) *Beyond beginnings: Literacy interventions for upper elementary English language learners*. Clevedon, UK: Multilingual Matters.

Dufficy, P. (2005) *Designing learning for diverse classrooms*. Sydney: Primary English Teaching Association.

Federal Race Discrimination Commissioner (2001) *Face the facts: Some questions and answers about immigration, refugees and indigenous affairs*. Sydney: Human Rights and Equal Opportunity Commission.

Garan, E. M. (2002) *Resisting reading mandates*. Portsmouth, NH: Heinemann.

Gibbons, P. (2002) *Scaffolding language, scaffolding learning*. Portsmouth, NH: Heinemann.

Guthrie, J. T. (2004) 'Teaching for literacy engagement'. *Journal of Literacy Research*, 36(1): 1–29.

Hedge, Trisha (2003) *Teaching and learning in the language classroom*. Oxford, UK: Oxford University Press.

McNaughton, S. (2002) *Meeting of minds*. Wellington, New Zealand: Learning Media.

NSW Department of Education and Training (1998) *Learning in a culturally diverse society: Consultation draft*. Sydney: Multicultural Programs Unit, NSW Department of Education and Training.

NSW Department of Education and Training (2002) *Students of non-English speaking background*, 2002. Sydney: Strategic Information and Planning Directorate, NSW Department of Education and Training.

Ogbu, J. U. (1991) 'Minority coping responses and school experience'. *Journal of Psychohistory*, 18(4): 433–456

Wallace, C. (1988) *Learning to read in a multicultural society: The social context of second language literacy*. New York: Prentice Hall.

Weizman, Z. O., & Snow, C. E. (2002) 'Lexical input as related to children's vocabulary acquisition: Effects of sophisticated exposure and support for meaning'. *Developmental Psychology*, 37(2): 265–279.

.... literacy-assessment practices profoundly affect what competencies are made visible to teachers and parents, and how particular students' literacy achievements are framed in discussion. .... if teachers are to be less constrained in what they notice and report about literacy achievements, they need support to scrutinise dominant assessment frameworks to debate different ways of understanding literacy, and to consider the potential consequences of these things for individual students in their school.

(Nixon, 2003: 107-108)

7 Authentic reading assessment

Assessment reveals what we value – we need new measures and 'new eyes' to note the important things young children understand.

(Connor, 2003: 72)

Ann Daly

Introduction

Assessment is an integral part of the reading program, and not something to add on afterwards. Its primary purpose is to improve student performance, and so assessment should be based on an understanding of how students learn. It is most effective when it reflects the fact that learning is a complex process that is multi-dimensional, integrated and revealed in student performance over time. There should be assessment *for* learning, as well as assessment *of* learning. Baseline diagnostic assessment of what students can and cannot do is needed *for learning*, to precede decisions about what should be taught. Assessment can act *as learning* when it is used to provide feedback and opportunities for student reflection and/or self-assessment to support future learning. Assessment *of learning* provides information about what students have learnt in relation to standards. Assessment should be an integral component of the teaching and learning process.

Traditional use of standardised tests

In the past, reading has been assessed by using standardised tests. These tests were usually *norm-referenced assessments* used to measure student achievement and progress compared to that of other students. Such assessments do not provide diagnostic information about the reading strategies that children use or whether students can apply these strategies in new situations. Nor do they assist teachers to assess their own teaching strategies. Clay (1993: 6) argues that standardised tests do not measure slow progress well and asserts that teachers can identify these particular children before the tests can effectively do so.

Normative assessments that rank students can only benefit the self-esteem of the top performing students, and yet they do not identify areas to further challenge these students and may in fact disadvantage them by encouraging them to be satisfied with current achievements. The same has been said of any form of assessment by grading (Keen, 2005: 24).

Other criticisms of most standardised tests in Australia are that they are linguistically and culturally biased in favour of Anglo, middle-class children, and that they only assess the reading of print on paper. The multimodal nature of reading in today's world makes standardised tests extremely limited in their relevance. Teachers need to be able to assess students' ability to read visual information in the form of moving pictures, diagrams, illustrations and photographs in books, e-books, CD-ROMs, DVDs, websites, television programs, films and videos. Even the ability to read written text is more complex than in the past, requiring different strategies for different formats such as email, CD-ROMs, websites and advertisements. The assessment of such a variety of reading strategies can seem daunting, but planning assessment as part of the teaching and learning process and using the Four Resources Model of Luke and Freebody (1999) makes the task manageable.

A simple example of the use of the Four Resources Model to analyse a visual text is provided by Sue Hamilton-Smith (2005) from Fitzgerald State School, where she gave each of her students a Mintie lolly, asked them to examine the wrapper and write their responses to the questions on the following page.

Code breaker	Text participant
How do I crack this code? What is on the wrapper? What colours are used? What lines are used? What layout is used? What framing is used?	*What does this text mean to me?* What does this text remind you of? What genre is this text? What story is the cartoon telling? What type of cartoon is this? Are there other types of cartoons? Compare this cartoon to others.
Text analyst	**Text user**
What does this text do to me? Why were the colours chosen? Why have a cartoon on a lolly wrapper? Would everyone find this joke funny? Who wouldn't buy Minties? Whose ideas are represented?	*What can I do with this text?* Write the story of the cartoon. Tell your 'It's moments like these ...' story. Write your own story. Draw your own cartoon. Find a text related to this text. Write the story as a news report.

Figure 1: Sample brainstorm questions using the Four Resources Model

The advent of an outcomes approach to the teaching of English in all states of Australia since the mid-1990s has made it possible, and in fact obligatory, for teachers to assess student achievement and progress against a standards framework. Such assessment is called *criterion-referenced assessment.*

Teachers should use formative, summative and authentic assessment for all aspects of learning in their classroom.

Formative, summative and authentic assessment

Formative assessment occurs when teachers teach differently in response to assessment data from their students. Formative assessments usually occur during teaching activities and are continuous. The student's performances on these assessment tasks are used by the teacher to make decisions about what to teach next in order to assist the student's learning. It is part of the teaching cycle and not part of grading. Formative assessment is even more valuable when it is used to give feedback. At the 2005 Australian Literacy Educators' Association Conference, in the Garth Boomer Address, James Gee advocated that teachers try to mimic the pedagogy of computer games because, among other features, "there is abundant formative feedback enabling players to monitor their learning and plan improvement" (Dooley, 2005: 6).

Summative assessment is the sum of judgements based on a range of assessment sources to determine what the student has achieved and learnt at the end of a unit of work or as a cumulation of a semester or whole year. Summative assessment is based upon the accumulated learning that has taken place over a period of time and can also be diagnostic in nature. Summative assessment should track progress against curricular targets and key objectives in a unit of work.

Authentic assessment is based on the development of a meaningful product, performance or process over time (also known as 'rich tasks' in Queensland). In authentic assessments, students develop and demonstrate the application of their knowledge and skills in real-world situations. This promotes and supports the development of deeper levels of understanding. Authentic assessment stems from clear criteria of which students are aware. In fact, students are often involved in the development and evaluation of the criteria as well. Students and teachers may also collect evidence of student development over time in learning journals or portfolios. The criteria for authentic assessments are often expressed in rubrics.

Assessment is an effective teaching tool when its function is formative. Diagnostic statewide assessment information is often regarded as only summative data, but its function can also be formative when it is used in conjunction with other information to carry out action research. For example, in Mendooran Central School in New South

Wales, "statewide assessment data was analysed to identify targeted students and highlight areas for specific literacy improvement" and then a middle years literacy project was implemented after reflecting on how the students best learn and "the success of the project was also measured against this data" (O'Rourke, Hill & McGirr, 2006). Similarly, at Hebersham Public School in Sydney's western suburbs, where students were performing below state average, the NSW Basic Skills Tests results were used to establish a baseline of diagnostic data (NSW Department of Education and Training, 2005). The data was used to determine student needs and develop appropriate teaching programs, which led to an increase in the literacy performance of students. To assist teachers with analysis, most states now provide data electronically, either in the form of data online (as in Victoria) or as reporting software packages (as in New South Wales and Queensland).

A comprehensive study of young students and their teachers (Louden & Rohl et al., 2005) demonstrated how effective use of assessment can improve student learning outcomes. Two of the teachers in the study were identified as being more effective than the others. One of the three main areas where their teaching was differentiated was their use of assessment. The greatest learning gains were made by the students of the teacher who had used assessment, provided challenge and encouraged student independence in literacy learning throughout her teaching practice. The other teacher orchestrated lessons well, and stimulated and engaged her students, but did not use assessment tools in the same way.

Formative assessment records are also important for future planning and reporting purposes. Within classrooms, teachers need to select assessment strategies that are appropriate to the outcomes they are teaching. Classroom reading assessment strategies can take the form of observation records, running records (see Chapter 5), self-assessment and reflection (often using rubrics and learning journals), teacher-designed questions or rich tasks/authentic assessments (often negotiated tasks with negotiated assessment criteria).

Observation records

Observation records are particularly valuable in the early stages of learning to read. Skills being observed at this stage might include book orientation (front to back, top to bottom, left to right) or recognition of individual words and letters. At any stage when a lesson has been planned, the expected syllabus reading outcomes can be listed on a matrix against the names of students. This matrix can be easily carried on a clipboard while teachers observe and support students. A tick for achievement of the outcome is easy to record, but it is advisable to allocate codes for other possible behaviours and to invent new codes as new behaviours are observed, to save time in recording. For some skills, observations can also take place across many activities, in a variety of settings, using a range of tools.

The observation records can be transferred to individual student records as an ongoing process of accumulating data for summative assessment. Observations can be recorded on proformas for specific purposes.

It is valuable also to include parents in observational assessments. For example, Anne Nelson, of Spensley Street School in Victoria, sends home a communication book:

> The parent or caregiver writes the date, title and a brief comment whenever the child takes a book home to read. Sometimes children write their own evaluative comments in here too.
>
> Anne: "I regularly write comments about the child's reading in here too, because it's part of my reporting process."
>
> *(Nelson, 2003: 77)*

Analysing reading: Running records and miscue analysis

Running records on their own are basically tests of accuracy and fluency in oral reading. They also can be used to determine whether a text is at an independent level for a particular reader – that is, it can be read with 95–100% accuracy (fewer than 5 errors) – or it is at instructional level (between 5 and 10 errors), or is below instructional level (more than ten errors) and therefore can be used for shared reading.

However, statistics about fluency and accuracy are not particularly useful on their own. Teachers cannot rely on oral reading accuracy as an indicator of reading comprehension, and it is important to note that some students (especially ESL students) can decode quite fluently but have little idea about the meaning of the text (see Chapter 6).

It is more useful to make a *miscue analysis* of a record of reading by making informed judgements about the student's specific needs related to the four sources of information being drawn upon: semantic (meaning), grammatical (structure or part of speech), graphological (visual) and phonological (sound). Dunn, Knight and Axtell (1993), who provide a comprehensive guide to miscue analysis, recommend using a tape recorder and a text of at least 400 words so that a minimum of 25 miscues can be analysed. However, Clay (1993: 24) states that shorter texts may be used at an early reading level.

When taking the record of reading, teachers record errors and omissions on their copy of the text. Self-corrections are noted (**sc**) but are not considered errors when completing the record of reading. Hesitations are also recorded but not analysed, as are repetitions, which are marked with an **R**, and any modification or assistance by the teacher, which is noted by a **T**. The teacher then categorises each error according to which of the four sources of information is causing difficulty for the student and places a cross in that column. Some people also record a tick in the other columns whenever the substitution is consistent with those sources of information.

Record of reading	Source of information (cues) used when making errors		
Cast Adrift	Graphological/ phonological (visual/sound)	Grammatical (structure/ part of speech)	Semantic (meaning)
/ / / / / / / / The little boat went floating across the river			
/ / / blows / / / / / and the wind blew it one way then the		X tense	
/ / landed around / (o) / other. Water lapped against the edges and	X around		X lapped
/ clods race / / / white clouds raced through the sky.	X 'o' for 'ou'	X tense	X clods
/ / dugout / / / / / / Soon the dinghy was in the middle of the	X dugout		
/ / they / waiting(sc) / / / river and there was water all around them.	X 'ey' for 'ere'	X subject/verb agreement (they was)	
/ call / / / / / hear Jason called for help but no one heard		X tense X tense	
exkept / kookaburs(sc) what / / except the kookaburras who replied with		X relative pronoun	X exkept
unseen laughing / / / / unseemly laughter. Susan began to cry.	X 'n' for 'mly' X 'ing' for 'ter'	X verb/noun	X unseen
/ / / / / / / Jason said that the kookaburras were only			
/ / chop / / / / / trying to cheer them up but she didn't	X 'op' for 'eer'		X chop
belive(sc) / / (o) / / / / believe him. Jason knew he would have to			
/ / / look / / / / / act fast. He looked for something to use as		X tense	
/ T a paddle.			X paddle

Note: Although many of the grammatical errors here involved good recognition of beginning sounds, they ignored final sounds on words.

Figure 2: Example of a teacher's miscue analysis

If analysis of a student's reading shows difficulty with graphophonics, it is worth remembering the advice of Helen Woodward (1987: 6) when planning teaching strategies: "always keep the letters in the context of the word and always keep the word in the context of the sentence" because children can often read words in context which they cannot read in an isolated list.

Running records are time consuming, but not all children will need regular monitoring through running records.

Self-assessment and reflection

Self-assessment is a powerful tool for empowering students to monitor their own learning and set goals for improvement. The quality of the self-assessment will depend on the tools, support and modelling given by the teacher (which will in turn depend on the age and skill level of the students), the way in which self-assessment is built into the learning process, the guiding questions asked, and the opportunity to regularly engage in self-assessment. Strategies for self-assessment may include:

- Reading logs/journals – keeping records of their reading and/or viewing allows pupils to keep track of what they have read and their reactions and feelings over time. Systematically kept and regularly used records can be examined by children who can then "begin to describe changes or lack of change based on information contained in the records" (van Kraayenoord, 2003: 48). Such records are also useful for teachers to consider so that they can suggest reading material that will interest students but also move them forward in their reading skills and literary challenges.
- Reflective journals – used to record students' reflections and growth as learners over time. To be meaningful and support students' learning, the journals should be completed on a regular basis, be integrated into the curriculum, form the basis of other activities such as learning journals, portfolios or triangulated interviews, and be valued by both the teacher and the student. Triangulated, or three-way, interviews between student, teacher and caregiver can provide valuable assessment information about student interests and family background, as well as being an effective means of reporting.
- Rubrics – these are definitions of a quality performance, requiring measurable criteria that are developed and provided 'up front' when an assignment is given. Rubrics clarify the task and help students to monitor their own learning. They provide a simple way of integrating assessment into the teaching rather than stopping the teaching to assess. Rubrics are particularly useful in rich tasks, which will be discussed later in this chapter, especially when the criteria are negotiated

between students and teachers. The following matrix in Figure 3 is an example of part of a rubric for a reciprocal reading group task (Bean, 2005: 8):

Reciprocal teaching	**3**	**2**	**1**	**Student**	**Teacher**
Predicting	My predictions were thoughtful. I used all the information available to me to make my predictions.	Most of my predictions were thoughtful, but at times I did not think about what I had read already when making new predictions.	I did not use the information available to me to make my predictions.		
Clarifying	I always asked for clarification of words I did not fully understand. I helped the group by clarifying terms for group members.	I did not always ask for clarification of words I did not understand and I did not always help the group when clarifying.	I often did not ask for clarification of words I did not understand. I did not offer suggestions to the group.		
Questioning					
Summarising					
Next time I am in a reciprocal teaching group I will ...					
Teacher comment:					

Figure 3: Part of a rubric for a reciprocal reading group task

Teacher-designed questions and statewide reading tests

These two different applications of assessment have been put together for two reasons. First, most statewide reading tests are designed by qualified teachers. Second, consistency of teacher judgement is a big issue that needs to be addressed across and between states, and so using the statewide tests as a model can assist in developing some consistency in assessment. The descriptions of skills and the questions used to assess these skills in the statewide tests can act as a standard against which teachers can develop their own questions and determine what constitutes achievement of a reading skill or syllabus outcome.

Most teachers are aware of three-level guides to questioning (3H strategy). Level one questions are about locating *literal* information HERE in the text, level two questions are about *inferential* information or what is HIDDEN between the lines, and level three questions are about reading beyond the lines (in the HEAD) and *applying and evaluating* information by relating it to their own background knowledge (NSW Department of Education, 1993).

Within each of these levels of questioning, there are more specific skills that need to be identified and assessed individually. Many of these skills are targeted in statewide reading tests. For example, some of the reading skills that are addressed by the NSW statewide tests include the ability to:

- connect information by following pronoun references and cohesive links;
- make connections between written information and visual images;
- make inferences that are implied in the text;
- interpret images, such as illustrations, photos, diagrams, maps, graphs;
- use and identify layout features and text conventions;
- recognise grammatical and text features;
- identify point of view, audience and purpose;
- identify the theme or main idea of a text or part of a text;
- identify the meaning of unfamiliar, technical, colloquial or figurative language from its context.

It is also important to analyse the miscues that students make when answering comprehension questions. For example, in a Year 4/5 class that included many experienced as well as struggling readers there was a general tendency to answer 'why' questions with 'what' or 'how' answers. One useful strategy was to introduce the class to Bloom's taxonomy and ask them to design different level questions based on this taxonomy for their peers to answer about a shared book. The strategy was successful with *all* students.

With regard to statewide tests, it is stated in the preface to the *Queensland Years 3, 5 and 7 Literacy and Numeracy Tests Reporting Handbook* (Queensland Studies Authority, 2005) that the tests should not be regarded as the sole literacy and numeracy assessment tool for students, and that they complement but do not replace other effective classroom assessment and reporting practices. Statewide tests do not pretend to assess all aspects of literacy, only some. Each is a one-off snapshot that parents and teachers can use to judge how their students are performing against the rest of the state.

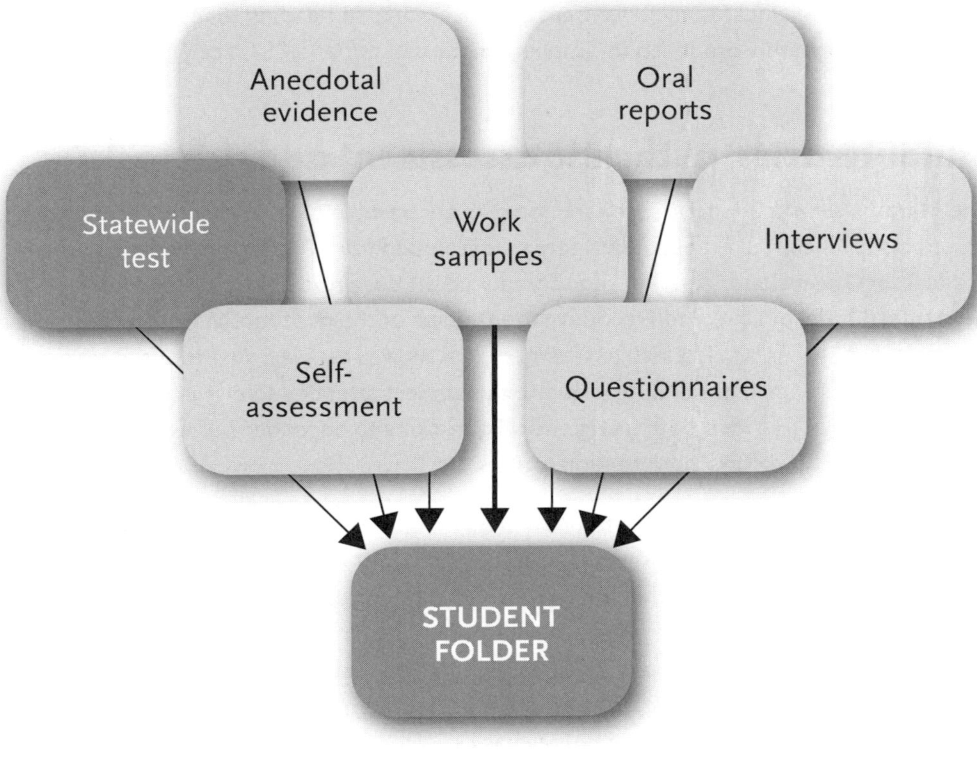

Figure 4: Placing the test results in context

In Queensland, principals and teachers are told that they "should confirm the test results with existing assessment data gathered by the school by means of observation, consultation and other formal statewide test instruments ... If, in some instances, the test results give a different picture, consider why differences may have occurred. The results of the tests may indicate some aspects of students' performance that may need further investigation within the classroom" (Queensland Studies Authority, 2005: 4). <http://www.qsa.qld.edu.au/testing/357tests/reporting_handbook.html>

It is worth noting the finding of Woods, Henderson and Hirst (2003) in their paper, *When deficit meets accountability*. Their research showed how external tests were sometimes more accurate than teacher assessments of students who had been incorrectly labelled low-achievers because of low expectations related to sibling behaviours or language difference or socioeconomic background.

The National Benchmarks in Reading, which are minimum standards for progression, are currently assessed by a cut-off score on each statewide reading test reporting scale. However, a national test for achievement of benchmarks in Reading, Spelling, Writing and Numeracy is currently proposed for implementation in 2007 (DEST, 2005).

Multiliteracies, authentic assessment and rich tasks

The *Marathon Project* (Healy & Honan, 2004) is an example of an authentic assessment, or rich task, which was mapped onto targets developed from Productive Pedagogies (Education Queensland, 2001). It monitored student development using the Four Resources Model of Luke and Freebody (1999). Each of the multimodal texts produced by a group of students was a rich assessment task as well as a learning event. With the Four Resources Model in mind, teachers in this project attended to eight critical framing principles, which included both using critical questions to engender self-examination of knowledge and using text interrogation targets.

Productive Pedagogies are part of the *New Basics Project* conducted by Education Queensland. The aim of this project is to connect student learning to local and wider community practices in ways that are purposeful and to prepare students for the future by dealing with new student identities, new economies and workplaces, new technologies, diverse communities and complex cultures. Figure 5 opposite outlines the New Basics triad and shows how rich tasks are the form of assessment used. <http://education.qld.gov.au/corporate/newbasics/>

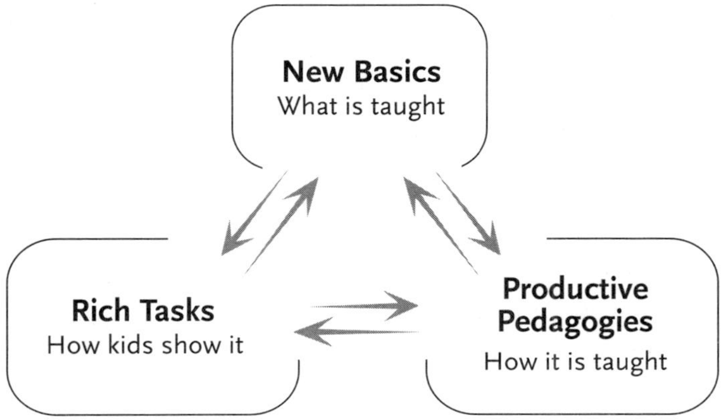

Figure 5: The New Basics conceptual framework

Other states in Australia are also developing new conceptual frameworks to show recognition of the need for reading, and literacy in general, to span all key learning areas and to cover many different forms of literacy – that is, to use multiliteracies pedagogy. Quality Teaching Frameworks (QTFs) and Comparative Outcome Groups (COGs) are being developed by the NSW Department of Education and Training. In Victoria, an even more comprehensive whole-school curriculum planning framework, the *Victorian Essential Learning Standards* for all schools from Prep to Year 10, has been developed and is to be implemented in 2006 <http://vels.vcaa.vic.edu.au/> . The South Australian Curriculum Standards and Accountability Framework (SACSA) is also conceptualising the learning attributes that students will need and has selected the headings *Futures*, *Identity*, *Interdependence*, *Thinking* and *Communication*, while the Tasmanian Essential Learnings Framework has identified the headings *Thinking*, *Communicating*, *Personal Futures*, *Social Responsibility* and *World Futures* (Fehring, 2005: 100).

Conclusion

Teachers need to be aware that students from poor communities, in particular Indigenous students, continue to have the lowest literacy performance of all, and the gap in achievement widens as these students get older. It is also notable that boys continue to have lower literacy achievements than girls. Badger and Wilkinson (2003: 65) point out that:

> the answer... 'is less about finding more technically efficient assessment tools and more about changing classroom literacy programs. As teaching and assessment are inextricably linked, teachers' programs have to provide the spaces and opportunities through which students can demonstrate the diversity of their literacy competencies'.

Alloway and Gilbert (2003: 175) warn teachers to "notice those whom we disenfranchise and disaffect", while, on the positive side of the issue, Comber and Kamler (2005) show the importance of parent interviews and independent assessment of students' social needs and interests leading to change in teaching practices and a turnaround in the outcomes for 'at-risk' students. The 'new measures' sought by Jenni Connor in her quote at the beginning of this chapter may in fact stem from new contexts, purposes and meanings that will be assessed within learning events that are relevant to students of different gender, culture or socioeconomic background to their teacher. The biggest assessment task of all for teachers is to assess their students' interests and backgrounds so that they can start from where students are at and make learning relevant to and meaningful for them.

References

Alloway, N., & Gilbert, P. (2003) Reading literacy test data: Benchmarking success? In H. Fehring (Ed.), *Literacy assessment: A collection of articles from the Australian Literacy Educators' Association*. Delaware, USA: International Reading Association, Inc.

Badger, L., & Wilkinson, L. (2003) Literacy assessment of students from poor and diverse communities: Changing the programs, changing the outcomes. In H. Fehring (Ed.), *Literacy assessment: A collection of articles from the Australian Literacy Educators' Association*. Delaware, USA: International Reading Association, Inc.

Bean, W. (2005) PEN 148: *Using rubrics to enhance student learning and self-assessment*. Sydney: Primary English Teaching Association.

Clay, M. (1993) *An observation survey of early literacy achievement*. Auckland: Heinemann Education.

Comber, B., & Kamler, B. (2005) *Turn-around pedagogies: Literacy interventions for at-risk students*. Sydney: Primary English Teaching Association.

Connor, Jenni (2003) Assessment: Profiling literacy with young Indigenous children. In H. Fehring (Ed.), *Literacy assessment: A collection of articles from the Australian Literacy Educators' Association*. Delaware, USA: International Reading Association, Inc.

Dooley, Karen (2005) 'On the beach again'. *Practically Primary*, Vol. 10, No. 3, October.

Dunn, M., Knight, B. A., & Axtell, J. (1993) PEN 91: *Unwrapping miscue analysis*. Sydney: Primary English Teaching Association.

Education Queensland (2004) *The New Basics Project*. <http://education.qld.gov.au/corporate/newbasics/>

Fehring, H. (2005) 'Critical, analytical and reflective literacy assessment: Reconstructing practice'. *Australian Journal of Language and Literacy*, Vol. 28, No. 2, June, 95–113.

Hamilton-Smith, S. (2005) 'Lolly wrapper literacy' (Practical strategies insert), *Literacy Learning: The Middle Years*, Vol. 13, No. 3, October.

Healy, A., & Honan, E. (2004) *Text next: New resources for literacy learning*. Sydney: Primary English Teaching Association.

Keen, S. (2005) 'Making the grade'. *Australian Educator*, No. 48, Summer.

Louden, W., Rohl, M., Barratt-Pugh, C., Brown, C., Cairney, T., Elderfield, J., House, H., Meiers, M., Rivalland, J., & Rowe, K. (2005) 'In teachers' hands: Effective literacy teaching practices in the early years of schooling'. A special edition of the *Australian Journal of Language and Literacy*, Vol. 28, No. 3, October.

Luke, A., & Freebody, P. (1999) 'Further notes on the four resources model'. *Practically Primary*, 4(2): 1–8.

Nelson, A. (2003) Authentic assessment and system accountability. In H. Fehring (Ed.), *Literacy assessment: A collection of articles from the Australian Literacy Educators' Association*. Delaware, USA: International Reading Association, Inc.

Nixon, H. (2003) Reassessing literacy. In B. Comber & J. Barnett (Eds), *Look again: Longitudinal studies of children's literacy learning*. Sydney: Primary English Teaching Association.

NSW Department of School Education (1993) *Choosing literacy strategies that work: Stage 2*. Sydney: Curriculum Directorate, NSW Department of School Education.

NSW Department of Education and Training (2005) *Hebersham Public School DVD*. Sydney: Professional Learning and Leadership Development Directorate, NSW Department of Education and Training.

O'Rourke, V., Hill, S., & McGirr, B. (2006) PEN 152: *Grammar games*. Sydney: Primary English Teaching Association.

Queensland Studies Authority (2005) *Queensland Years 3, 5 and 7 Literacy and Numeracy Tests Reporting Handbook*. Brisbane: Queensland Studies Authority.

Woods, A., Henderson, R., & Hirst, E. (2003) 'When deficit meets accountability'. *Wordsworth*, (36) 4.

Woodward, H. (1987) PEN 63: *Reading problems: More phonics?* Sydney: Primary English Teaching Association.

van Kraayenoord, C. E. (2003) Toward self-assessment of literacy learning. In H. Fehring (Ed.) *Literacy assessment: A collection of articles from the Australian Literacy Educators' Association*. Delaware: USA: International Reading Association, Inc.

In a digital age, literacy education has responsibilities to engage students in learning contexts using knowledge processes that prepare them for an ever-evolving text landscape. Literacy practices must be as responsive to new media as to the concept of world audiences.

(Healy, 2004:6)

8 Using ICT for learning to read and write in the early years

Jan Turbill

The use of technology in early years classrooms is not new. We have had pencil and paper for many years, and before that chalk and slates. The many books that can be found in early years classrooms are also considered a form of technology. These paper-based materials too have changed in appearance, type, quality and quantity over the years. Go into any early years classroom, and teachers will be using whiteboards and markers, as well as the traditional chalkboards. Then, of course, we find all the electronic technology such as overhead projectors, pencil sharpeners, tape recorders and listening posts, CD players, and, in some classrooms, even DVD players. And now, almost all early years classrooms have at least one computer, while some have data projectors and interactive or 'smart' boards.

Computer technology has opened up different modes of communication, which are commonly known today as 'information communication technologies' or ICT. The use of ICT and the computer have certainly changed my life, and the way I both access and provide information. It has become my preferred 'tool' for writing, as well as for communication with friends, family and colleagues. My 'snail' mail has almost disappeared, and my telephone use has also decreased. My whole way of thinking has been changed by the advance of ICT.

While it was evident that my experiences were reflected in many homes and offices throughout Australia, it also became apparent from my involvement in schools in the late 1990s that this was not the case in the average classroom. I was interested to find out why. I was particularly interested in finding out how teachers of young children were attempting to incorporate technology into their literacy programs – and if not, why not. And so I began a research project that has spanned some six years now. Using a multimode methodology of case study (Yin, 2003) and action research (Kemmis & McTaggart, 1988), I have interviewed teachers, children and parents. I have observed teachers in action during their daily literacy block. I have gathered video data of five year olds 'playing' at the computer using CD-ROM 'stories' such as Talking Books, reading programs such as Galaxy Kids, and software such as KidPix, iPhoto and PowerPoint.

It has been a long, slow, but interesting process that has created an enormous amount of rich data. Initially, my research focused on 'mapping the territory' through interviews with early years teachers and through observations of them teaching during their daily literacy block.

Mapping the territory

My early analysis of teachers' views during this phase can be best summed up by a Kindergarten teacher's comment: "Having one computer in the room with 25 Kindergarteners is as useful as having one tin of pencils". She went on to say, rather sheepishly, "If I had my preference, I would sell the computer and buy more books". I learned some major 'lessons' from the final analysis of these early interviews and observations (Turbill, 2001a & b). These lessons can be categorised as follows.

Computer-related lessons

Computer-related lessons include the need for the computers to work, to have access to a printer, the internet, digital cameras, and so on. Teachers found it very frustrating when the computers did not work for whatever reason. Many had little knowledge of computer use beyond being able to open a Word document or an internet browser. However, if, for instance, the icon to either of these programs disappeared from the desktop, most were unable to navigate their way around the directories to find the original application.

While there is often a person in the school who is designated as the 'computer person' and given release time to help with computer problems, my research found that this person was usually kept very busy with the issues of the more senior classrooms, or was simply not available at the point of need. For instance, Wilma, a Kindergarten teacher, was about to show the children how to use KidPix. All the children were sitting facing the computer screen, eager to 'have a go' themselves. Wilma turned on the computer, thinking aloud and using the appropriate terminology as she did so. What happened next was quite unexpected, and Wilma was quite flustered as to what to do. It was obvious that KidPix had loaded, but only one third of the program could be seen on the monitor. The rest seemed to have disappeared. Wilma had no idea what to do, and so the planned lesson was scrapped and the likelihood of her using the computer again in her literacy block was slim. What had happened, we discovered, was that 'little fingers' had played with the monitor buttons, and the 'screen' had been moved sideways. We both learned that a simple adjustment would have quickly fixed the problem. However, for this teacher, it was a long time before she was prepared to risk using the computer again.

Software-related lessons

Suitable software, and time to explore such software, is a major issue for early years teachers. My research found that teachers knew little about the software that was available, and those who had seen software "that looked interesting" in catalogues had little or no idea of what might be involved in its use. Sustained time is needed to explore the potential use of software and new programs. The lack of such time was cited as a major issue.

Curriculum-related lessons

This group of teachers questioned whether they needed the additional technology to teach literacy anyway. They felt they had been successfully teaching children to read and write using traditional technologies such as paper and pencils, and therefore questioned the 'value added' through using technology. It was clear that this group of early years teachers (and I suspect most others) held a traditional view of literacy that was based on a paper-based/print-based pedagogy of literacy, and that these views would need to be challenged if change was to ever take place.

Teacher-related lessons

Teachers themselves felt apprehensive about how to use computers, and those who did use them for their own personal and administrative purposes could not see the potential other than 'play' within their existing framework of what constituted literacy teaching and, particularly, how it was best taught. They also found it difficult to organise the use of the computers when there were 26+ children, two computers and one teacher.

What to do next?

Many of the key points that emerged from these 'lessons' still exist. However, it became increasingly apparent that most teachers of early literacy view ICT as something that their students can 'play' with during 'free time' or as a 'reward' after the real 'work' has been completed. Even though many teachers of young children are now quite skilled in using

ICT for their personal and professional purposes, there seems to be a reluctance for many reasons to integrate the technology into their classroom literacy practices.

Thus, while there is much written about embedding ICT into the classroom literacy curriculum, I propose that many teachers of young children still operate within the paradigm that literacy is a set of skills to be mastered, and that technology is an additional tool that does not necessarily enhance the literacy learning of young children.

I am not alone in these beliefs. In their federally funded review of teacher professional development in the area of ICT across the K–12 perspective, Downes et al. (2001: 58) concluded that despite an "enormous investment in ICT-related continuing professional development" there was little evidence of change that went "beyond the act of embedding ICT into existing curriculum to the act of transforming curriculum frameworks (both pedagogies and content)". Furthermore, they suggest that professional development should be reframed "within a package of curriculum reform, pedagogical reform and a redefinition of the teaching profession as one of knowledge generation" (p. 77). Downes et al. quote the 1996 OECD study *Changing the Subject*, which states that in order to achieve the benefits of technological innovations:

> ... teachers will have to change almost every aspect of their professional equipment. They will have to reconsider themselves entirely – not only the structures of their material and their classroom techniques, but even their fundamental beliefs and attitudes concerning learning.
>
> *(Black & Atkin, 1996: 63)*

Contemporary views define literacy as social practice (Muspratt, Luke & Freebody, 1997; Makin & Jones Diaz, 2002; Zammit & Downes, 2002; Harris, Turbill, Fitzsimmons & McKenzie, 2006, to name a few). Thus, in today's classrooms literacy pedagogy should incorporate those practices that we use to communicate and function in our everyday lives, including the computer, internet, email, CD-ROMs, DVDs, digital cameras, and so on.

Zammit and Downes (2002: 24) propose that:

> Literacy can no longer be seen as just a set of cognitive abilities or skills based on an identifiable technology, for example, alphabetic script on paper. It needs to be recognised as a social activity embedded within larger practices and changing technologies.

Such a broadening of what constitutes literacy and literacy practices clearly has implications for literacy pedagogy in the first years of school.

Zammit and Downes (2002) agree that a more contemporary view of literacy must include a far more diverse and complex set of texts and technologies. Thus, learning to be literate using such texts involves more than simply adopting the paper-based skills into the new environments. It requires adapting known skills, as well as learning new skills (Labbo

& Reinking, 1999; Lankshear & Snyder, 2000; Leu & Kinzer, 2000; Zammit & Downes, 2002). Such learning, it is argued, must begin with the emergent and beginning readers and writers (Labbo, 1999 & 2000; Labbo, Sprague, Montero & Font, 2000; Labbo & Kuhn, 2000; Turbill 2001a).

The challenge therefore becomes how can teachers best include ICT in their existing literacy program without it being seen as an 'add-on' or simply 'play'. How can ICT become embedded into a teacher's pedagogy and the everyday classroom practices of young children? Enter a simple classroom approach called Digital Language Experience Approach (DLEA).

Digital Language Experience Approach

Digital Language Experience Approach is clearly described by Labbo, Eakle and Montero (2002). Their research indicates that "as promising as recent research and instructional ideas have been, we realized that much remains to be learned about effective ways to integrate LEA [Language Experience Approach] with digital photography and creativity software in the early years classroom".

Language Experience Approach is an approach I had used in my teaching of Kindergarten and Grade 1 students back in the early 1970s. It is based on the premise that if children could tell their 'story' and someone could scribe that story for them, then they would be able to 'read' it (Ashton-Warner, 1963). It was, and still is, a very successful teaching method. Teachers and students create class booklets as well as individual Language Experience booklets. Children either draw a picture and the teacher scribes a caption to accompany it, or the child offers the caption first and then draws or paints a picture. The 'stories' created can be used to teach children phonics, high-frequency words, punctuation, and much more. LEA can include Modelled Writing as the teacher scribes a child's or children's collaborative story, thinking aloud about the processes of how to spell the words, rereading the text, and so on. Class libraries fill with the children's books, and the stories are read and reread by students.

It is an approach that has been found to be particularly useful for ESL students who are beginning to learn English and English script. It is one of the many teaching approaches in the teaching of reading and writing in the early years that is still used with many variations in most Australian classrooms today.

Certainly the early years teachers in whose classrooms I had been researching used LEA in their daily literacy blocks. They had indicated to me often that they felt comfortable using such traditional teaching approaches, and yet they also were aware that they needed to somehow incorporate the computers they had in their rooms into this teaching. Incorporating a digital component into LEA seemed a logical and non-threatening change.

Adopting Labbo et al.'s (2002) work as a base, the following components were changed or introduced:

- All teachers had access to PowerPoint, and many had used it in their own work or in university studies, thus it was felt that this software would suit our purposes better than the creativity software such as KidPix used by Labbo and her colleagues.
- Children would take the lead and would select the photos they wanted to take with the digital camera (after Espinetti, 2002).
- Where possible, children would be encouraged to compose and write their own 'stories' or captions, rather than the teacher or volunteer scribing the story, as is the case in Kindergarten.

After some initial staff development for teachers on using PowerPoint to create a slide show, using a digital camera, uploading digital images from the camera and then downloading them into PowerPoint, we were ready to begin. In what follows, I share a cameo that is a compilation of two teachers' endeavours. For the purpose of the cameo, I shall call this fictitious teacher Mrs Denny.

Cameo: Mrs Denny introduces DLEA into the literacy block

When DLEA was introduced at the staff development day in Term 1, Mrs Denny felt that it not only sounded like a great idea, but it also was something that she could achieve, given her limited use and understanding of technology and the two computers in her classroom. Furthermore, she had always used LEA, but had found the children's drawings of the scribed message were usually so immature that they were unlikely to help children to remember what the print might say. Children therefore seemed to quickly lose interest in using these LEA books. Mrs Denny believed that using digital images that all the children had experienced would be far more effective, especially with her many non-English speaking background students.

The first DLEA book was created during the first week of school. Mrs Denny took five photographs of the children at various times on the very first day. These were inserted into PowerPoint and shown to the children during that same week. At this stage no text was added. Mrs Denny and the children simply reflected on and talked about their first day of school.

During the second week of school, the children and Mrs Denny created a caption to go with each of the slides. Since they had been talking about the photographs each day, the children were able to talk quite freely about each one. Mrs Denny steered the children towards the creation of a caption that reflected the major time episodes of a school day. For instance, "*At 11 o'clock we go outside for little lunch and play*", and "*We all go home at 3 o'clock*". The captions were first written on the chalkboard as a modelled writing demonstration. Later, a parent helper copied them onto the matching PowerPoint slide. The children were shown the PowerPoint slide show, entitled *Our Day in KD*, and they attempted to 'read' along with Mrs Denny. Five hard copies were made, and the cover sheet was laminated. The children had their first digital and paper-based book. They proudly 'read' their book to anyone who came into the room. Because the photographs were recognisable to them, and because they had already talked a great deal about them, many of the children confidently 'read' the text as well. Some made up additional bits, but the children always talked about the photographs.

In week 3 of Term 1, Mrs Denny gradually introduced the digital camera to small groups at a time. The plan was to create a digital book that introduced all the children, entitled *We are in KD*. Individual children were asked to photograph their friend (with the support of Mrs Denny). Many photographs were taken by the end of the week, with many of the same child; however, Mrs Denny made sure that each child had been photographed. During week 4 two children from KD's Buddy class in Grade 5 uploaded the photographs and deleted all those that were out of focus or too skewed. The Buddies called each child in turn to come and choose the photograph of themselves (if there was more than one) to be inserted into PowerPoint. The children also watched as the older child inserted their photograph and wrote the sentence, *I am* ... Each child was expected to help with the writing of his or her name. For instance, when writing *I am Zibu*, Zibu went to his desk and brought back his name card and pointed to each letter as the older child wrote it.

By week 5, the class had two digital books with paper-based versions. The paper-based versions were included in the 'Take Home Reading Program'. Mrs Denny was thrilled with the children's response. They loved their digital books and wanted to use the computer to read them. 'Reading' the digital books became a group activity, with pairs of children working at the computer at the one time. Paper copies were also printed off using the school's colour printer, and these were displayed around the room. Mrs Denny reported with great excitement that the children were going around the room and reading the text under each photograph.

Next, Mrs Denny began a unit of work on colours. Each week saw a different focus on a colour. The many activities through the week culminated on Friday with the children wearing something in the week's colour, as well as cooking something in that colour. For instance, in Green Week, the children, with the help of the teacher and a parent helper, made celery boats. Celery sticks cut into 3 cm pieces were filled with cream cheese, and a toothpick was stuck into the cream cheese to form the mast. They also had frozen green grapes and green apples.

Digital photos were taken of the 'cooking' and eating part of the day. These photos were uploaded into PowerPoint – one photo per slide with no text. Mrs Denny, with the help of some of the children, viewed these in the 'slide sorter' and chose six slides that best represented what had taken place. Mrs Denny then ran off four sets of the slides with no text. During group work in the literacy block of that week, Mrs Denny asked the group to form a circle around the sheets that she placed on the floor. The children were then asked to order the images to best represent the sequence of events as they remembered them during Green Week.

What was evident for each group was that because the children had been part of the experience, the photographs jogged their memories, and they were willing to talk about them. Mrs Denny recognised the potential benefits for children from ESL backgrounds when they are given more opportunities to talk about shared experiences such as these. Once the children had decided on a sequence, they helped the teacher to compose a caption for each slide. The children watched as Mrs Denny wrote their caption. As she did this, Mrs Denny often stopped to:

- point out particular letters;
- ask if anyone had that letter in their names;
- talk about the sound of letters;
- explain English syntax, such as plurals, verb endings;
- suggest words.

For instance, when one of the groups came to the slide about the frozen grapes, one child offered the word 'cold' to describe the grapes. Mrs Denny accepted 'cold', but went on to tell the children that there was a word in English to describe something that was "very very cold – so cold that we say it is 'frozen' ". The caption then became "*We ate frozen green grapes*".

Each group developed their digital version of Green Week. The captions were written onto the PowerPoint slides, and the class then had four new digital books. Printed copies were made, and children could choose to read the screen version or the paper-based version. Each group took great pride in reading their version to the class. The recounts of what happened during Green Week now became useful reading material. Children happily revisited their digital books. For this class, it also meant that they were immersed in English structures and vocabulary.

Mrs Denny created an additional digital book using the existing Green Week photographs in order to introduce the children to procedural texts. Entitled *How to Make Celery Boats*, the text was as follows:

You need:

- A bunch of fresh celery
- A sharp knife
- A packet of cream cheese
- Some toothpicks

Take the bunch of celery and break the stalks off.
Get the celery, knife and cream cheese ready.
Cut the green stalks into 3 cm pieces.
Put a teaspoon of cream cheese in the celery.
Place the toothpick in the cheese for the mast.
Eat the celery boat.

Again, both digital and paper-based books were made available for the class. Furthermore, the digital books now could be shared easily among all Kindergarten and Grade 1 classrooms by putting them onto the school's intranet. Because the photographs were common images, children could talk about them, add to them, or even write their own captions and create a personalised slide show. Children loved to see the photos of themselves and their friends on the computer, and, as predicted, children wanted to read the 'digital books' over and over again. Thus, children and teacher were beginning to use ICT for authentic purposes, and not just as something to do when the children finished their 'real' work.

By the middle of the school year, Mrs Denny had learned that there were many features of PowerPoint that she could use with the digital books in order to teach the children skills needed for reading and writing. For instance, the class developed a digital book entitled '*What I like to do at school*'. With 15 captions and photos (some children had common 'likes'), Mrs Denny created three separate digital books. The captions in one book were:

I like to paint at school.

We like playing with the blocks.

I like to read books on the computer.

I like to write on the chalkboard.

In each of the digital books, Mrs Denny was able to display the individual words on the bottom of the slide in the form of 'flash cards'. At the first mouse click, the word '**I**' appeared. At the next mouse click, '**I**' faded in colour and '**like**' appeared, and so on until each word had been shown. At the end of the book, individual words were placed on the slide, such as '**like**', '**to**', '**we**', and so on.

In another version, Mrs Denny was able to highlight letters and their sounds by changing the colour of the letter with a mouse click. In yet another version, Mrs Denny created a cloze by deleting a word. For instance, '*I _ _ _ _ to paint*'. Children were given a paper copy and had to fill in the missing word.

By the end of the year, KD had many digital books on the school's intranet. The books were used for many purposes and were now very much part of the literacy block. Children and teacher were also becoming confident users of the technology. Their ICT skills had developed and certainly expanded beyond the use of playing CD-ROMs. Children from the Buddy Grade 5 class had shown teacher and children how to find images on the internet and download these for their digital book on *Australian Animals*. It was not unusual during discussions to hear the children say, "Let's Google it and find out". Mrs Denny admitted that ICT was very much part of her literacy program, and would continue to be. "I can't teach without it now!" she was heard to say.

Conclusion

It would seem that for early years teachers to recognise literacy as "a social activity embedded within larger practices and changing technologies" (Zammit & Downes, 2002: 24), they need to see how their existing successful practices can be enhanced through the use of such technologies. DLEA is one of many ways that may assist in this transformation. Certainly, once the process begins and success is experienced, as with Mrs Denny, the possibilities are endless.

References

Ashton-Warner, S. (1963) *Teacher*. New York: Simon & Schuster.

Black, P., & Atkin, J. (1996) *Changing the subject: Innovations in science, mathematics and technology education*. London: Routledge/OECD.

Downes, T., Fluck, A., Gibbons, P., Leonard, R., Matthews, C., Oliver, R., Vickers, M., & Williams, M. (2001) *Making better connections*. Canberra: Department of Education, Science and Training, Commonwealth of Australia.

Espinetti, G. (2002) 'Images that capture stories of our worlds: A new literacy for preschoolers'. Paper presented at the International Reading Association Conference, San Francisco.

Harris, P., Turbill, J., Fitzsimmons, P., & McKenzie, B. (2006) *Reading in the primary schools years* (2nd ed.). Sydney: Thomson Social Science Press.

Healy, A. (2004) 'Multiliteracies pedagogy'. *Practically Primary*, June, 9(7): 6.

Kemmis, S., & McTaggart, R. (1988) *The action research planner* (3rd ed.). Victoria: Deakin University Press.

Labbo, L. (1999) 'A semiotic analysis of young children's symbol making in a classroom computer center'. *Reading Research Quarterly*, 31(4): 356–385.

Labbo, L. (2000) '12 things young children can do with a talking book in a classroom computer center'. *The Reading Teacher*, 53(7): 542–546.

Labbo, L. D., Eakle, A. J., & Montero, M. K. (2002) 'Digital Language Experience Approach: Using digital photographs and software as a Language Experience Approach innovation'. *Reading Online*, 5(8), May. Accessed 30/3/2006 at: <http://www.readingonline.org/electronic/elec_index.asp?HREF=labbo2/index.html>

Labbo, L., & Reinking, D. (1999) 'Negotiating the multiple realities of technology in the literacy research and instruction'. *Reading Research Quarterly*, 34(4): 478–492.

Labbo, L. D., Sprague, L., Montero, M. K., & Font, G. (2000) 'Connecting a computer center to themes, literature, and kindergarteners' literacy needs'. *Reading Online*, 4(1), July. Accessed 30/3/2006 at: <http://www.readingonline.org/electronic/labbo/>

Lankshear, C., & Snyder, I. (2000) *Teachers and technology: Managing literacy, technology and learning in schools.* Sydney: Allen & Unwin.

Leu, D., & Kinzer, C. (2000) 'The convergence of literacy instruction with networked technologies for information and communication'. *Reading Research Quarterly*, 35(1): 108–127.

Makin, L., & Jones Diaz, C. (Eds) (2002) *Literacies in early childhood: Changing views and challenging practices.* Sydney: Maclennan and Petty.

Muspratt S., Luke, A., & Freebody, P. (Eds) (1997) *Constructing critical literacies: Teaching and learning textual practice.* Sydney: Allen & Unwin.

Turbill, J. (2001a) 'A researcher goes to school: The integration of technology into the early literacy curriculum'. *Journal of Early Literacy*, 1(3): 255–279.

Turbill, J. (2001b). 'Getting kindergarteners started with technology: The story of one school'. *Reading Online*, 5(1), July/August. Accessed 30/3/2006 at: <http://www.readingonline.org/international/inter_index.asp?HREF=turbill2/index.html>

Yin, R. (2003) *Case study research: Design and methods* (3rd ed.). Thousand Oaks, CA: Sage.

Zammit, K., & Downes, T. (2002) 'New learning environments and the multiliterate individual: A framework for educators'. *Australian Journal of Language and Literacy*, 25(2): 24–36.

The overall mandate, as I see it,
is to ensure that students leave
each level of schooling with a
developed and reflective sense of
their own reading strategies, with
a range of insights into how
texts work, and with an array
of strategies for resisting, contesting
and re-writing texts.

(Corcoran et al., 1994:23)

9 Designing challenging reading strategies for students in the middle years

Bill Spence

Acquiring reading knowledge and skills is a lifelong process. It is not something that ends when students master the mechanics of reading. To meet the requirements of syllabuses in the upper primary and early secondary years, students need to be able to read a wider range of texts for an ever-increasing variety of purposes. Students need explicit teaching, guidance and support to increase their repertoire of reading strategies to enable them to deal with the increased complexities of these texts.

What do skilled readers do?

When planning for reading instruction that best supports students' development of effective skills and strategies, it is useful to reflect on what skilled readers do.

The main strategies and understandings displayed by skilled readers are that they:

- set themselves a clear purpose for reading;
- use a variety of reading techniques, such as scanning for key facts and rereading important sections, dependent upon the purpose of their reading;

- seek to gain an overview of the text prior to reading in order to note which parts of the text are the most important for their needs; and
- constantly evaluate and make interpretations about what they are reading, linking new information to their prior knowledge.

Purposes for reading

One important strategy that is used by skilled readers, and that can be taught to all students to assist them in understanding what they are reading, is for them to have a clear purpose for why they are reading each text, and to keep this purpose in mind during the reading session.

Texts for different subjects may require different reading strategies. Some topics may require the reading of large amounts of information, and so it is necessary for students to quickly cover the whole text and select the sections that might be the most useful. Other topics may require closer, more intense reading of smaller amounts of text. It is necessary for students in the middle years to know how to:

- **browse** – this involves students getting a general overview of a text to gauge if it might contain the information that they are looking for (browsing may include looking closely at the cover, name/s of author/s, back cover blurb, and contents and index pages, as appropriate);
- **skim** – this involves a more detailed checking to gauge if the book contains the information needed (skimming may include locating headings and subheadings, and looking for key words in relevant sections); and
- **find facts** – this involves a close reading of the sections of text that look the most likely to contain the information sought.

What makes a text easy or difficult for readers?

The vocabulary used in texts that middle years students are required to read is generally technical and specialised to the topic. The language is concise, with a lot of information 'packed' into complex sentence structures. The texts will often contain graphics such as diagrams, tables and photographs that require students not only to interpret their meaning, but also to connect this meaning to the written text and synthesise the meaning constructed through the interplay of the written text and the graphics.

Teachers can assist students' understanding of the texts they are required to read, first by analysing how the texts are structured, and second by incorporating explanations of these constructions into pre-reading activities. Features of texts that can act as barriers to understanding include:

- the vocabulary used, particularly the number and frequency of the technical words that are specific to a topic;
- the structure of the text, including the use of guides such as headings and subheadings, and the length and complexity of sentences, paragraphs and chapters;
- the types of graphics used to impart meaning, their complexity and their alignment with the ideas and concepts in the written text; and
- the complexity of the new ideas and concepts, and the degree to which they are explained and/or linked to known knowledge.

It is critical to look carefully at the texts that students will be required to use and to consider what features of the texts may affect their reading. This may be for all students, particular groups or individual students.

Sometimes the option may be to select an easier text, but for many topics this may not be possible. Explicit instruction and guided support by the teacher or more experienced reader can make even quite challenging texts accessible to students. Strategies that can be used to provide this instruction and support are listed below.

Strategies for teaching reading in the middle years

While the strategies described below can be used across a number of school years and for students at different levels of reading ability, they have been selected because they are particularly useful in supporting readers who have mastered the fundamentals of reading but still need explicit teaching to support them as they tackle more difficult texts.

It is important that the strategies are explained explicitly and then demonstrated to students before they are expected to use them effectively themselves. Students in the middle years not only need a range of reading strategies that they can draw upon, but they also need to be able to select the most appropriate strategy for their reading purpose. Students can be encouraged to do this by being asked to consider:

- Why am I reading this text?
- What do I want to know?
- How is the information organised in the text?
- Do I need to read all of the text or just some sections?
- What reading strategy will help me find the information I need?

Before reading

It is important to have students reflect upon what they already know about a topic before they commence reading. Prior knowledge, gained from previous studies or life experiences, contributes strongly to students' ability to understand a new text. Teachers can assist students to activate their prior knowledge by encouraging them to talk about what they already know and by providing opportunities for them to begin linking their prior knowledge to the new concepts and ideas.

Brainstorming

Brainstorming is a means of activating all knowledge known about a topic. Students are asked, either individually, in pairs, or in small or class groups, to list all that they know about a topic they are about to study. Students can be encouraged to include vocabulary, facts, concepts and questions covering what they would like to know more about.

It is important to document brainstorming sessions (e.g. chalkboard/whiteboard; computer/smart board; audiotape; wall chart; mindmap in students' notebooks) so that the information can be returned to at a later date in order to assist students to make links from their prior knowledge to new knowledge and also to show them the learning they have made.

The information from brainstorming sessions also can be used to encourage students to begin making connections between what they already know. Students can organise the information by grouping items according to common features, and then give each grouping a heading.

Predicting

Predicting involves students considering and discussing what they expect they will be reading about in the new texts. Asking students to anticipate what they might be learning is a powerful tool to activate prior knowledge and to motivate enthusiasm and interest for reading.

Predictions can be stimulated by showing students the cover, telling them the title, or displaying text features such as headings, subheadings, pictures, and graphics such as maps, graphs and diagrams, and then asking them to predict what they think the text might be about. After students have made their predictions, have them check the Contents or Index pages to confirm their predictions or to revise them if necessary.

When reading literary texts, it is useful to encourage students to stop at different places in the text, generally at the end of chapters, to reflect on what they have read and to predict what might happen in the next chapter. Asking students to predict the content prior to reading also provides them with a purpose for reading, as they will be keen to check to see if their predictions were accurate.

Structured overview

A structured overview involves students gaining a cursory understanding of how the information is structured in the text before they begin reading. Students are asked to skim through the book, noting structural architecture such as title, chapter headings, main headings and subheadings, and any bolded words or phrases.

If needed, these could be recorded to act as a summary of the book and as a guide to locate sections that might contain information the student is specifically looking for.

Graphic overview

A graphic overview is a summary of the graphic, or visual, elements of a text. Graphics might include illustrations, photographs, graphs, diagrams, maps, and so on that provide information other than what is contained in the written text. It is important to make students aware that the graphic component of texts often contains information that helps illustrate the written text, but it also can contain information not included in the writing. To miss, or not comprehend, the information contained in graphics may lead to a misunderstanding of the overall concepts treated in the text.

Students can compile a graphic overview by starting at the beginning of a text and listing the types of graphics contained in it, including the content covered by each graphic. Table 1 is the beginning of a graphic overview of a book about the planet Earth.

Table 1: Example of a graphic overview

Page	Type of graphic	Content
3	timeline	The development of Earth
5	photograph	The solar system
6	photograph	The Sun
8	diagram: cross-section	The planet Earth
9	photograph	A meteorite
10	map	Continental masses
11	illustration	The oldest known fish
12	photograph	A fossil found in Western Australia
14	illustration	Prehistoric life on Earth

As well as making students aware of the information contained in graphics, a graphic overview can also serve as a quick reference guide to locate information in the text.

Key words

When preparing students for the study of a new topic, it is important to make them aware of the new words they might come across when reading texts about the topic. These new words may be the technical language or vocabulary specific to that topic, or may be other vocabulary that is unfamiliar to them.

It is important, when presenting key words for the first time to students, that the words are presented in activities that allow students to understand the meaning of the words within the context of the topic. For example, the word 'disk' has a number of meanings, but only one that is specific to the topic of computers.

Before reading an unfamiliar text, students can be asked to skim the text and list the words that they are unfamiliar with. Before checking the meaning of each word in a dictionary, the students can be encouraged to guess the meaning, based on how the word is used in the text, and the context of the words around it. Table 2 shows the headings of a worksheet for the documentation of this activity.

Table 2: Sample worksheet headings for identifying the meaning of key words

Word	My guess, based on context	Dictionary meaning

During reading

While students are reading, it is important that they are aware of strategies they can use to monitor their understanding of the text and, if necessary, use to improve their understanding.

Directed reading

Directed reading involves the teacher asking questions about a passage that students are about to read. The students then read the text to locate the answer. Directed reading gives the students a purpose for their reading. The strategy can be used with a whole class or smaller groups. After students have been given time to read and find the answer to the question/s, the teacher can then lead a discussion that clarifies the answer/s and allows students to share their understandings.

It is important that students are told within what part of the text the answer is located. The number of questions asked and the extent of the passage that needs to be read to locate the answer/s can vary with the reading ability and concentration span of the group.

Comparing texts

As mentioned earlier in the chapter, it is important that students realise how their understanding of a text is often dependent upon them synthesising the information they have read in a written text and the information gained from the graphics or visual text accompanying the writing.

Students can be asked to divide a page into two columns and list the facts they have learnt from reading the written text in one column, and the facts taken from any graphics in the second column. This page can then be used for a class or small group discussion based on questions such as:

- Where was the most information contained?
- Did the visual text support the written text?
- Was the information contained in the visual text a repeat of the written text or did it extend the written information?

Talking the text

The overuse of technical language, long complex sentences, and sentences packed with lots of dense noun groups are often quite typical of the style of writing in texts that middle years students are required to read. Talking out the text is a whole-class or small-group strategy that focuses on encouraging students to rephrase the language of the text in their own words.

Led by a teacher or another more experienced reader, students are asked to read a section of a text and then are asked questions that focus on them having to explain the technical vocabulary or phrases in everyday language. Students are encouraged to build on each other's responses and to link the new learning to prior knowledge, understandings and experience.

Post-reading

After reading a text, it is critical that students participate in strategies that require them to review their understanding of what they have read and relate any new knowledge to prior understanding or previously acquired background knowledge. This can be done successfully by having students revisit the text to answer questions, make judgements on opinions and concepts in the text, or apply the information they have learnt to other contexts.

Summarising and note-making

An effective way of ensuring that students have understood what they have read is to ask them to present a summary of the key information – the main points – in their own words.

One way of doing this is to ask students to make a list of key words while they are reading. When they have finished reading, they can use these words to form sentences. There is less chance of the students' sentences being an almost exact copy of the original text if:

- a period of time is left between the reading and the writing of the summary; and
- the original text is not available to the students when they are constructing their summary.

Table 3 details the headings on a worksheet used to encourage note-making.

Table 3: Sample worksheet headings for note-making

Text:	
Key words	**Sentences**

Re-forming the text

Re-forming involves students presenting the information they have gained from their reading in another form. For example, information from a written text could be presented as a diagram, as an oral report, a PowerPoint display, visually as drawings or illustrations, or as a performance piece such as a play or a dance drama.

The decisions that have to be made by students when selecting and ordering the information they are using to construct the other form generally involves the use of higher-order thinking skills such as evaluating and synthesising.

Response journals

Response journals encourage students to reflect on their understandings by having them write about, for example, what they have learnt, what it means to them, how they might use the information, and what additional information they still need to locate.

Students should be encouraged to make brief entries in their reading journals prior to reading, and to respond after reading in order to clarify and reinforce their understanding. The following can act as prompts to stimulate response journal writing:

- Was the reading easy or difficult? Why?
- What reading strategies did I use? Were they successful? Why or why not?
- What strategy might I try next time?
- My strongest reading skills are ...
- I am not as good at ...
- I need to practise ...

Comprehension

Comprehension is the ability to make meaning from a text – to understand what has been read. There are varying levels of comprehension, beginning at a literal understanding of the content and developing to a critical understanding where the student gains an awareness of the author's ideas, concepts and purposes for writing the text, and is able to evaluate this within a framework of their own views, knowledge and understandings.

The more sophisticated texts that students in the middle years have to read require them to go beyond literal understandings. It is important that students are provided with explicit instruction in a range of comprehension strategies and opportunities to practise the strategies in a variety of contexts.

Strategies for teaching comprehension in the middle years

Questioning

Effective questioning can help students by guiding them to the important sections of a text as they read to locate the answer.

It is important that students are asked a variety of types of questions, not just questions that ask only for a literal answer, or an answer based only on facts contained in the text. There have been many different attempts to categorise types of questions (see, for example, Good & Brophy, 2003; Orlich et al., 2004). In addition, Bloom's taxonomy (1956) is often cited when considering different levels of questions.

Table 4 lists three levels of questioning that extend from literal understanding to more higher-order thinking.

Table 4: Sample worksheet showing three levels of questioning

Questioning technique	Level of understanding	Example question stems
reading the lines	factual – can be answered directly from text	Who ...? Where ...? When ...?
reading between the lines	inferential – encourage students to interpret the information	What are the differences between ...? Why ...? Explain ...
reading beyond the lines	applied – encourage students to evaluate and apply the information	What are some possible solutions to ...? Explain how ... What do you think about ...? Can you support ...?

Students need explicit instruction in what the different levels of questioning require of them and how they might answer them. Posing a question and asking students to work with a partner to locate and formulate an answer before discussing potential answers with a larger group is one good strategy. Students need to be made aware of the fact that many questions do not have only one answer and that good answers often are based on how the reader interprets the text and the author's messages.

Once students have an understanding of questioning, particularly the higher-order levels, they should be provided with opportunities to write their own questions and give them to other students to answer. Hotseating or group questioning in role (Ewing & Simons, 2004) is very effective when probing characterisation and can be undertaken after the questions are formulated. The discussions held between the question writer and those answering the question are often very rich and are always based on their understanding of what they have read.

Using graphics to organise information

Constructing graphics such as tree diagrams, wheel diagrams, timelines and flow charts are great ways for students to show the relationships between the information and concepts in a text. Brady (2006) provides some useful examples of different kinds of graphic organisers based on earlier classification of these by Pohl (1997).

Different types of texts lend themselves to different kinds of graphics. For example, a timeline is a good way to represent the information from a biography, and a tree diagram is usually suitable for an information report. Encouraging students to try different ways, and then giving them time to share their work with other class members, encourages discussion about text information and further allows time for them to clarify their own interpretations. Students will begin thinking about suitable ways of graphically presenting information when they are asked to draw or sketch a picture that illustrates key facts or concepts.

The reverse of this strategy, and another way of supporting students' understanding of what they have read, is to ask them to present an important graphic in written form. Writing about the information contained in, say, a graph or a diagram can be quite challenging, and it demands a high level of understanding of the information contained in the graphic.

Jigsaw

Jigsaw is a strategy that is useful for texts that can be divided easily into a number of sections. Individual students, or a small group of students, are given one section. The student/group has to read their section and summarise it in preparation for joining with students who have read the other sections. It then becomes the responsibility of each student to instruct the others about the information contained in the section they read. The larger group then has to make sense of the totality of the text.

This is a particularly good activity for mixed ability classes as students experiencing difficulty with reading can be paired with more able students or can be given an easier section of the text.

The jigsaw concept can be extended by giving students, pairs of students or small groups different books on the same topic and allowing them time to read and reflect on the reading, and then share and discuss with others. Each student, pair or small group could be asked to present a summary of their text. These summaries could take a variety of forms and could include oral presentations, PowerPoint displays, or graphics such as diagrams and flowcharts.

Conclusion

The role of the teacher in explaining and modelling the strategies covered in this chapter is critical. It cannot be assumed that students in the middle years will be equipped to read the texts required of them just because they have learnt the mechanics of reading in earlier years. As mentioned earlier, the complexity of the texts in the upper primary and junior secondary years demands different and varied reading strategies of students, and these need to be taught explicitly.

It is also important that students are provided with opportunities to practise these strategies in all key learning areas, not just in English. The literacy demands of all subjects will require students to read a variety of texts for a diverse range of purposes, and teachers again need to explain and model where and why different strategies are the most appropriate.

The prime focus of the teaching of reading in the middle years should be to provide students with a broad and diverse range of reading and comprehension strategies so that they have choices they can draw upon as they approach new and challenging texts.

References

Bloom, B. (1956) *Taxonomy of educational objectives: The classification of educational goals. Handbook 1: Cognitive domain*. New York: David Mackay.

Brady, L. (2006) *Collaborative learning in action*. Frenchs Forest, Sydney: Pearson.

Corcoran, B., Hayhoe, M., & Pradl, G. (Eds) (1994) *Knowledge in the making: Challenging the text in the classroom*. Portsmouth, NH: Heinemann, Boynton/Cook.

Ewing, R., & Simons, J. (2004) *Beyond the script Take 2: Drama in the classroom*. Newtown, Sydney: Primary English Teaching Association.

Good, T. L., & Brophy, J. (2003) *Looking in classrooms*. Boston, MA: Allyn and Bacon.

Ministry of Education (2002) *Learning through language*. Wellington, New Zealand: Learning Media.

New South Wales Department of School Education (1997) *Strategies for reading factual texts*. Sydney: Curriculum Support Directorate.

New South Wales Department of School Education (1997) *Teaching reading: A K–6 framework*. Sydney: Curriculum Support Directorate.

New South Wales Department of Education and Training (1999) *Continuity of literacy development Years 5–8*. Sydney: Curriculum Support Directorate.

Orlich, D., Harder, R., Callahan, R., Trevisan, M., & Brown, A. (2004) *Teaching strategies: A guide to effective instruction*. (7th ed.). Boston: Houghton Mifflin.

Pohl, M. (1997) *Teaching thinking skills in the primary years. A whole school approach*. Victoria: Hawker Brownlow.

A Proper Little Lady

Times are changing, and fast. Our society is marked by the effects of globalisation and ever-increasing diversity of culture and language. Adding to the pace of change are the proliferating multimedia and information technologies. These phenomena are shaping the way in which meaning is created and exchanged, and they are generating a dynamic plurality of texts.

(Kalantzis, Cope and Fehring, 2002:1)

10 Teaching primary school children how to 'read' images

Alyson Simpson

Introduction

English has been described recently as the part of schooling where students "develop knowledge, skills and understanding about English language and literature, and the ability to talk, listen, read, view and write with purpose, effect and confidence" (DEST, 2005). There is a commonality suggested in this description between reading and viewing, since both modes of communication involve decoding and interpreting. It is clear also that in many texts there is a dependent relationship constructed where the image and written text are interrelated (Board of Studies, 1998; Simpson, 2005). Yet, much more time has been devoted to giving children an explicit awareness of how written texts are constructed than to teaching them how to 'read' images.

This chapter addresses the topic by giving examples of how images in picture books, factual texts and online narratives can form the basis of pedagogically sound teaching practice. The example lessons show how giving children a metalanguage with which to discuss images – that is, a visual literacy – enables them to demonstrate deep understandings about how texts work.

To demonstrate the link between written text and visual literacy, try to complete the puzzles below by considering both what the words say and where they are placed. Hint: they are well-known sayings.

STEPS STEPS PETS	Time Time	The CARPET SWEEP

Tricky isn't it? You probably thought about the meaning of the words before you used the significance of the placement of words to help you decode the text. Yet, in order to recognise the meaning being constructed, you needed an understanding of verbal *and* visual literacy. In other words, it is both the written text and the visual layout that is important in reading and understanding these messages.

If we accept that when we read icons/symbols we 'decode' shapes, then we may wonder how, without any formal training, we have learned to read the combination of a curved line, two dots and a circle as the symbol . The answer may be a combination of context, experience and scaffolded support. This is a simple image, and so, as the majority of texts that primary school children deal with in classrooms today are a multimodal combination of written and visual elements, we need to reframe our approach to the teaching of reading images. We need to give students the scaffolded support of explicit teaching about visual literacy. We need them to recognise that reading images depends on understanding the importance of shape, layout, the relationship between elements that create the whole, the interpretation of colour, and so on. Reading visually is a complex process. Where letters represent sounds, the elements of images may simultaneously represent action/emotion/symbolism/classification/social importance/emphasis etc.

Theorists argue that devaluing visual literacy is not a balanced attitude as it ignores an important meaning-making resource.

> ... children actively experiment with the representational resources of word and image, and with the ways in which they can be combined. Their drawings are not just illustrations of a verbal text, not just 'creative embellishment'; they are part of a 'multimodally' conceived text, a semiotic interplay in which each mode, the verbal and the visual, is given a defined and equal role to play.
>
> *(Kress & van Leeuwen, 1996)*

In this chapter, I argue for a deeper understanding of visual grammar that enables teachers and students to develop their knowledge about how to read images. In order to achieve this aim, we need to teach students that images have a semiotic system and a grammar. We can show them that there are choices to be made within the grammar that will construct different meanings or different versions of 'reality'. The next section suggests a strategy that is useful in starting the discussion about how we construct and interpret images.

Developing a visual grammar with students

To start the discussion, illustrate the following sentences and then discuss with your students what understandings about images drove the choices you made when you drew your pictures.

Image 1	Image 2
The wind is blowing the leaves from the trees.	*My Year 4 class has 20 students in it with 15 girls and 5 boys. Two of the boys have red hair and three of the girls have black hair.*

Figure 1: Action or concept?

When you discuss this activity, you will find that different people have different words for the same idea. They know that in order to show leaves moving, they have to use lines or curves to imply movement. They know that in order to represent groups and differences, it is easier to use graphs or charts than draw each figure individually. In other words, what they are 'talking out' is the difference between active and abstracted imagery. The trouble is, without a grammar or vocabulary in common, you do not have a shared metalanguage that enables you to talk about images. With a visual grammar, we can shift from making general descriptions of images to creating informed critique (Simpson, 2004). One visual grammar that is currently available (Kress & van Leeuwen, 1996) allows us to distinguish between the two images by their purpose and would name Image 1 as *narrative* and Image 2 as *conceptual*.

Kress and van Leeuwen's grammar[1] is a highly sophisticated description of how visual design works. However, their grammar is not common knowledge, and it was not devised to be taught to young children. It was designed to mirror in parallel the different strands of meaning-making resources as identified by Halliday (1994) in his functional grammar

[1] See Appendix 1 for a summary of key concepts of Kress and van Leeuwen grammar of visual design.

of spoken and written language. The mapping of the visual grammar makes use of the same three strands of meaning as for written texts, but naming them for the purpose of distinguishing between verbal and visual: *representational*, *interactive* and *compositional* meanings. This means that a student can learn the resources through which material events, social relationships and semiotic structures are realised in visual grammar.

The following three case studies illustrate the work of teachers who are trying to bridge the gap between the theory of visual design and a child's understanding of image. Although each text and teaching context is different, all examples are related by the fact that they represent educators coming to terms with how to teach a grammar with only the beginnings of a metalanguage to describe it. It is interesting to note the different levels of technicality used and the 'commonsense' terms that creep into use when nothing else is available. In each case, it was clear that young children were able to deal with core concepts of visual grammar as they talked about images in their own terms.

Case study 1 – Reading and viewing: Interactive resources in e-texts

The context of the first case study is a series of lessons designed for children aged 8–10 years. The teacher uses visual grammar to support their lesson on e-texts (interactive books that are read on the internet). She wanted her students to attend to the ways in which images and words contribute to the meaning of the text as a whole. The e-text she used was called *The Final Quest*. (Note: While that website is unfortunately no longer online, the same topics could be applied to the *Spy Watch* site that is currently online at: <http://www.stmichaelscemidd.rochdale.sch.uk/subjects/english/spywatch/lar/index.htm>.)

The e-text in this case was a narrative, and so the teacher could have taught students how images can represent action and characterisation, can create a 'reading path' within a text or can construct social relationships between the viewer and the characters. For the case study below, she chose the last option. The images viewed in the lessons, such as the wizard and the wolf, were used to illustrate how social distance creates character–character and/or reader–character connections. Because the e-text context is an interactive setting, it includes an additional element that is missing from printed picture books – that is, the element of physical movement. The fact that characters could approach or move away from the viewer was important to the children's appreciation of engagement.

Learning experience

For the lesson that introduced the term *demand*, students first worked through the e-text, interacting with characters where necessary, and then observed how the characters moved and where they looked. After this step, the students discussed how in every screen shot the characters always looked directly at the viewer. The teacher then showed them a series of photographs and other images from books where characters or real people looked away from the viewer. The term *offer* was introduced to name this technique. The third step to the lesson was to ask students to discuss the contrasting effect of the two approaches on their emotional response to the image.

The teacher then introduced the concept of *social distance* by asking the students to consider how 'close' they felt to the characters in the e-text, both physically and emotionally. Who did they care most about, and why? When did they feel less connected to a character, and why? Students were asked to review the e-text and consider the visual techniques that had been used to guide their feelings. The questioning and the teacher's rewording of the concept in everyday terms were designed to encourage critical awareness of text construction.

A practical task required students first to convert two images that had been 'demands' (participants looking directly at the viewer) into 'offers' (not directly looking at the reader/viewer), and then increase the 'social distance' of the character from the viewer. They then discussed the resulting change in effect. This activity encouraged students to realise the importance of demand plus intimate social distance to create reader/viewer involvement.

The final assessment of a written comment under their own images was used to judge whether students recognised the effect of offer plus impersonal social distance to position the reader/viewer as an observer, and whether students realised how the importance of key characters was created.

The teacher designed consolidation of new knowledge as a concluding activity. Students were given magazines and asked to find contrasting images that clearly represented the visual techniques of demand/offer and social distance in use. They were then told to write words that symbolised the effect of the image on them as readers/viewers. For example, writing in large print if the image was a close-up shot:

demand = "friendly greeting"

and small print if the image was a long-distance shot:

offer = "forgotten friend"

The posters were then used as the basis of a rounding-off discussion.

Teaching terminology

The teacher rationalised her choice of the elements *contact* (offer/demand) and *social distance* as being important to the students' understanding of how the narrative works. The phrases 'looking at us' or 'staring straight at us' and 'not looking at you directly' were initially used to direct the students' observations of character eyeline. As student awareness grew, the information words were reframed into the technical terms *demand/offer* and *gaze*. The terms *social distance* and *positioning* were introduced in relation to feelings of 'connection', both physical and emotional, when characters 'were close to them' or 'come up to your face' in contrast to when they were 'far away'.

Children's vocabulary

The concepts of *demand* and *offer* were generally understood, which was evident when students were questioned about examples of demands in the text and they responded with comments such as: "I know this part in the book where the troll looks straight at you as if to say, 'I know who you are'." The teacher did not record students' use of the metalanguage, but reported that the introduction to visual grammar worked well in her opinion. The student work sample in Figure 2 below illustrates one student's understanding of *offer* in contrast to the more powerful social strategy of *demand*. This student had remarked earlier that the wizard was "staring straight at you like he knows you", and the image created demonstrates the contrasting view. This example demonstrates the student's comprehension of the concept of *contact*.

Figure 2: Work sample demonstrating one student's understanding of the term 'offer'

Case study 2 – Reading and viewing: Symbolic resources in a picture book

The context of the second case study was a composite class of 10–12 year olds. The image in Figure 3 below is a work sample that students completed after working through the lessons on visual literacy. Although it is a written text, it 'illustrates' the students' understanding of key terms concerned with symbolism in images. The lesson sequence was designed to compare how illustrators use symbolism with the way that writers use metaphor to create mood or signify meaning.

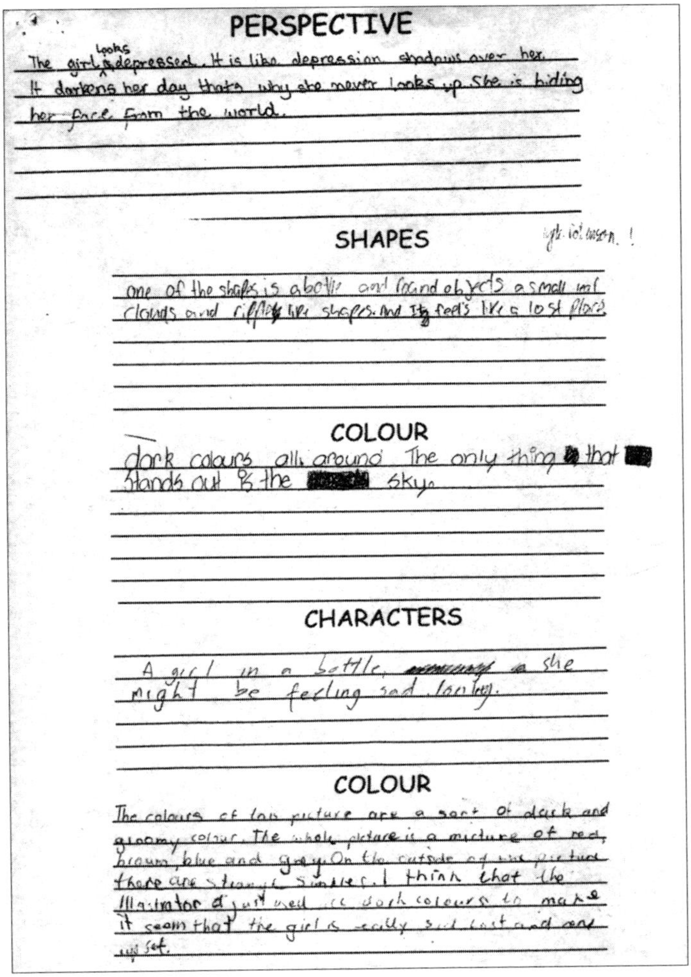

PERSPECTIVE

The girl looks depressed. It is like depression shadows over her. It darkens her day thats why she never looks up. She is hiding her face from the world.

SHAPES

one of the shapes is a bottle and round objects a small and clouds and ripples like shapes. And it feel's like a lost place

COLOUR

dark colours all around The only thing that stands out is the sky.

CHARACTERS

A girl in a bottle, she might be feeling sad, lonley.

COLOUR

The colours of the picture are a sort of dark and gloomy colour. The whole picture is a micture of red, brown, blue and grey. On the outside of the picture there are strange squiggles. I think that the illustrator just used dark colours to make it seem that the girl is really sad lost and are upset.

Figure 3: Work sample demonstrating students' understanding of symbolism in images

Learning experience

Prior to the sequence of lessons reported below, the students had read and discussed the novel and the film of the book *Bridge to Terabithia* (Paterson, 1978). They had examined how the author had used similes and metaphors to portray characters' emotional states. This work formed the main part of a sequence of 12 lessons on feelings and friendship. After working with the written texts, the students were introduced to the picture book *The Red Tree* (Tan, 2001), and their attention was drawn to the techniques used in images to portray emotions. The work on visual literacy was used to complement and extend students' critical understanding of modes of communication in narrative texts.

In an introductory activity focusing on emotion through imagery, students initially were asked to think about the words they would use to describe positive and negative aspects of friendships. They then examined the cover of *The Red Tree* and predicted the outcome of the 'story' in comparison to *Bridge to Terabithia*. The book was then read and discussed in terms of themes and emotional levels.

The next move in supporting students to apply their critique to images was to explain to them some technical terms for the techniques that illustrators use. These were represented as a scaffold (Callow, 1999) and included the terms *colour, perspective* and *shapes*. Small groups were formed, and each was given the task of examining a picture for its visual features. The groups wrote down their impressions and then presented them to the whole class.

To consolidate the learning, students were asked to present either a readers' theatre or a mimed version of the text. In order to achieve this successfully, the students needed to empathise with the characters and therefore respond to the emotional symbolism of the images. The teachers created an alternative version of the text that signalled a positive message. This new version was written as a contrast to the negative tone of the original. The new format was created deliberately to challenge the students to consider optimistic outcomes to sad situations. The assessment of their work was dependent on their portrayal of emotion through facial expressions or voice tone.

Teaching terminology

The terms *colour, shape, perspective, action, character, composition* and *setting* were used to describe how emotion could be portrayed in general. A more explicit focus was given to the symbolic use of colour and shape. These were investigated in terms of light and shade, brightness and darkness, and the meanings associated with particular colours, e.g. red vs. grey. Directions such as "Look at other colours and their impact" led the students into discussions of different interpretations of colours.

This work also led to awareness of cultural difference, providing a valuable learning experience. As with colour, shape was also treated in depth so that students would notice the regular use of circles and other naturalistic shapes. Students were then asked to consider the contrasting impact of angular, more industrial shapes in the images. The students were reminded that the illustrator was making deliberate choices to construct a meaningful picture. The teachers asked them: "What does the illustrator want to tell us through the artworks?"

Children's vocabulary

As the terminology for the focus lesson was based on 'everyday' words such as *colour* and *shape*, the students did not need to learn new word definitions. This meant that they were able to apply the terms for *description* and for *critical comment* quite quickly. For example, they could name colours used in the images – "red, brown, blue-grey" – and also give an interpretative response.

The students' written work samples illustrated how they applied the new visual literacy concepts they had learned, such as *colour, shape, perspective, symbols*, to the unfamiliar context of creating an interpretative reading of the images in a picture book: "I think the illustrator just used all dark colours to make it seem that the girl is really sad, lost and very upset".

The teachers were pleased by what they called the students' "impressive" application of the terminology in the discussion and feedback session.

Case study 3 – Reading and viewing: Coding orientation in factual texts

The context of the third case study is a plan for a unit of work designed for a class of 9–10 year olds. Figure 4 on page 134 shows a student teacher's model of the outcomes she expected would result from her lessons on visual literacy. Her choice of stimulus image signals the focus on coding orientation that her lessons are designed to teach. She has selected this feature of visual literacy as it facilitates students' learning in the integrated English and Science unit she has written about living things.

UNIT: FROGS

Answer the following questions:

1. Write a list of features about this image that you would change to make it look naturalistic.

- Take the smile off the frogs face
- Put the frog in a real life setting and add a background
- Make the frog look 3D
- Use correct/realistic proportions
- Use different types of green
- Some areas of the frog may be different colours
- Use light
- Make some areas brighter than others
- Add an action
- Make the fogs skin shiny to symbolise moisture

Fantastic Ellie 10/10

2. Would this image be useful in learning about a frog's diet and why?

This image would not be very useful because:
- It does not look like a real frog
- The image does not have anything to do with the kinds of food that a frog eats, how it eats, how it catches its food or where it finds its food.

3. Explain what type of background you would add to support a naturalistic image of a frog in its real life environment.

I would add a rainforest type background (trees, leaves, ponds etc.) using the sorts of colours found in its natural environment (greens, blues and browns).

Figure 4: A student teacher's model of expected outcomes from a unit of work on visual literacy

Learning experience

The first stage in the sequence was to introduce students to the topic of living things, which was also linked to the concept of the natural environment. A multimodal CD-ROM was chosen to show the students information about frogs in an interactive manner. The class was directed to consider the design of the CD-ROM and the title, and to predict whether the information would be realistic, i.e. reliable. As the images on the CD included both naturalistic and schematic examples, the teacher's initial focus led students quite easily into a discussion of the terms *realistic* and *unrealistic*. Students were challenged to justify what they based their opinions on, given that the social purpose of the CD is to act as an information resource.

Following on from the general discussion, a particular screen shot from the CD was displayed of a frog eating a snake. This image could be analysed according to the key elements the teacher had selected to teach, such as colour, setting and dimensionality. In a modelled teaching situation, students discussed how each of the attributes contributed to the overall meaning of the visual text. The teacher's aim was for students to recognise what makes something 'look real'.

A follow-up activity to consolidate learning was included in the sequence where students searched for and identified both realistic and unrealistic images from the CD. These images formed the basis of a guided session where students identified a naturalistic image and analysed the elements that made them think it looked 'real'. They then discussed which sort of image would best suit an information report.

To consolidate and assess individual learning, students were asked to independently critique the image shown on the worksheet in terms of its schematic elements. They had to list the features they would use to turn it into a realistic image. They were then asked to explain what background details they would add to the image and why, according to the purpose of the information report. The teacher was looking not only for the correct terminology, but also a sound rationale for each element chosen. Her work represents a good model of integrating English with Science through explicit teaching about visual literacy.

Teaching terminology

The terms *naturalistic* and *unrealistic* were used to describe the difference between real-life images and those that had been rendered in a more *schematic fashion*. The teacher recognised the role that *colour*, *setting* and *lighting* play in creating an effect, but chose to employ those terms in her discussion of *coding orientation*. She asked questions such as: "Which image is more like what you would see every day?" The technical term *degree of saturation* was not used in her explanation of naturalistic tones; rather, she recommended speaking about colours being *shiny* or *dull*. As her aim was to lead students into an awareness of the purpose of factual images to support information reports about living things, she wanted them to consider the elements that contribute to realistic portrayals of animals. Therefore, visual literacy elements such as *setting* were important as they place the living things into a realistic environment. To assess their understanding, the students were asked to apply their knowledge to an image that was schematic (see Figure 4).

Children's vocabulary

The terminology for this group of students included some technical terms that the teacher decided to translate: e.g. *schematic* = *unrealistic, degree of saturation* = *shiny or dull*. Because this lesson series was not actually trialled, we do not have examples of children's vocabulary use. The plan shows that the teacher would use questions to scaffold the students towards recognising the differences in the details. Both in-class discussion and the written assessment item would allow the teacher opportunities to observe evidence of student learning.

Conclusion

The case studies in this chapter serve to demonstrate how teachers are explicitly supporting students working with visual literacy. All three studies show how learning to read images has been contextualised for a meaningful purpose. Each teacher chose as their focus a different feature from the range of meaning-making resources used in images. They then interpreted the technical terminology according to the age level of the children and their prior knowledge of visual literacy. Thus, their teaching was informed by theory and appropriately matched the needs of the students. Individually, the case studies present examples of teachers and students finding ways of talking about images without the support of a systematic scope and sequence. Collectively, they represent an attempt to raise the importance of teaching students how to read images.

A search for a metalanguage of visual grammar in curriculum documents such as the *English K–6 Syllabus* (Board of Studies, 1998) shows that the list of terms is limited to: *Colour*, *Setting*, *Position*, *Direction*, *Size*, *Angle*, *Light*, *Symbolism* and *Point of View*. They do not appear schematised as a grammar, but are scattered within the document. When these terms are arranged into a visual grammar schema according to the three metafunctions (see Appendix 1), it is possible to see that there are insufficient terms available to sustain a complex analysis or even a balanced view of images. The best represented metafunction is the interactive, which means there are more ways of looking at how images connect with the viewer than there are ways of discussing what is happening in the image or how the image is logically organised.

So where does that leave us? We are in a position to recognise that teachers could be working with images, but we also recognise that there is no child-friendly metalanguage printed ready to use in a curriculum document. In order to move from this stalemate position, I suggest that the challenge for teachers is to work with students and images now without an official scope and sequence, but with the knowledge that images are worth critical attention (see Appendix 2 for a staged example to work through yourself). If teachers are informed by a sophisticated version of a visual grammar, then they will recognise when children use their own language to describe certain elements of the grammar. These new terms then can be incorporated into a class vocabulary for talking about images.

If we take the time to build an understanding of the core concepts, as well as a useable scope and sequence for a metalanguage for visual grammar, we will be empowering students by recognising the significance of their 'common' knowledge. In addition, we will be paying more appropriate attention to the sophisticated multimodal texts that are now so much a part of our everyday lives. In this context, grammar will be learnt not "as an end in itself, but as a means of improving students' abilities to use language more effectively and evaluate other texts critically" (Board of Studies, 1998).

The rationale behind working towards a visual grammar to support reading and viewing texts has never been to create a prescriptive, traditional grammar. My aim has been to create an explanation with student-centred examples that can be shared so that not only the structure of images can be discussed, but also so that their social implications may be critiqued. For, as Kress and van Leeuwen (1996: 45) remind us:

> Pictorial structures do not simply reproduce the structure of 'reality'. On the contrary they *produce* images of reality which are bound up with the interests of the social institutions within which the pictures are produced, circulated and read. They are ideological. Pictorial structures are never merely formal: they have a deeply important semantic dimension.

The next logical step is for us to reflect on the link between a detailed attention to a language of visual images and the kinds of discussion that it makes possible. If we consider the examples of teaching in this chapter, we can see that students are able to make much more critical evaluations of the construction of symbolism, point of view and notions of reality because the availability of a language literally enables them to make abstractions. Without explicit teaching, there can be no such discussion.

References

Board of Studies (1998) *English K–6 Syllabus*. Sydney: Board of Studies NSW.

Callow, J. (1999) *Image matters: Visual texts in the classroom*. Sydney: Primary English Teaching Association.

Department of Education, Science and Training (DEST) (2005) *Teaching Reading: Report and Recommendations*. National Inquiry into the Teaching of Literacy. Canberra: Commonwealth of Australia.

Halliday, M. A. K. (1994) *An introduction to functional grammar* (2nd ed.). London: Edward Arnold.

Kalantzis, M., Cope, B., & Fehring, H. (2002) PEN 133*: Multiliteracies: Teaching and learning in the new communications environment*. Newtown, Sydney: Primary English Teaching Association.

Kress, G., & van Leeuwen, T. (1996) *Reading images: A grammar of visual design*. London: Routledge.

Paterson, K. (1978) *Bridge to Terabithia*. London: Gollancz.

Simpson, A. (2004) 'What happens when a book gets judged by its cover? The importance of a critical understanding of images in children's picture books'. *Book Bird*, (3): 28–36.

Simpson, A. (2005) 'Four roles for the viewer? Developing an understanding of visual literacy'. Pleasure, Passion and Provocation: AATE/ALEA National Conference, July, Gold Coast.

Tan, S. (2001) *The Red Tree*. Port Melbourne: Lothian.

Acknowledgements

Thanks to the student teachers who were willing to share their classroom practice. Extracts from their work are displayed in the case studies. I acknowledge here the work of: Dimity Kremydas, Ellie Stanford, Magno da Silva and Betty Corolis.

Appendix 1

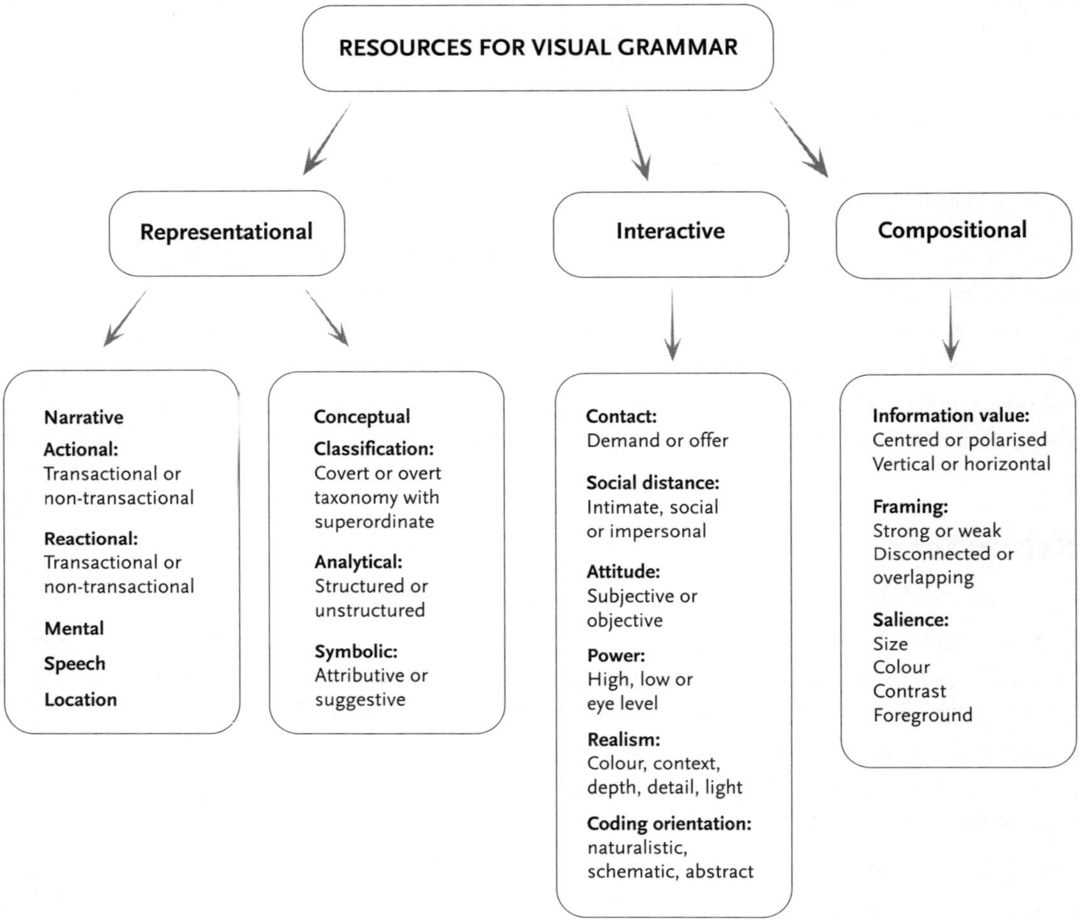
RESOURCES FOR VISUAL GRAMMAR
Representational
Interactive
Compositional
Narrative
Actional:
Transactional or non-transactional
Reactional:
Transactional or non-transactional
Mental
Speech
Location
Conceptual
Classification:
Covert or overt taxonomy with superordinate
Analytical:
Structured or unstructured
Symbolic:
Attributive or suggestive
Contact:
Demand or offer
Social distance:
Intimate, social or impersonal
Attitude:
Subjective or objective
Power:
High, low or eye level
Realism:
Colour, context, depth, detail, light
Coding orientation:
naturalistic, schematic, abstract
Information value:
Centred or polarised
Vertical or horizontal
Framing:
Strong or weak
Disconnected or overlapping
Salience:
Size
Colour
Contrast
Foreground

Appendix 2

Reading and viewing: Case study 4

The three case studies in Chapter 10 demonstrated teachers working with realistic or fictional images (conceptual or narrative). The fourth case study is a reflexive exercise where you are asked to consider what would be relevant to your classroom context. The stages of the task will be set out for you as a sequence of headings. Fill in your answers using short statements following the examples in the chapter.

Context

Age of class/group:

Focus text:	Choose an image that is relevant to your class. It may be factual or fictional.
Purpose of lesson:	Choose a feature of the image that you want to use to demonstrate how images work for a particular social purpose.
Learning experiences:	What teaching/learning activities would help you unpack the image and engage the children with concepts?
Teaching terminology:	What grammatical features would you pick and what language is appropriate with your group?
Children's vocabulary:	What terms are the students likely to use?

Questions for reflection

1. What language did Kress and van Leeuwen use to talk out your concept?
2. What language is there in the syllabus to talk out your concept?
3. What language did you use to talk out your concept?
4. Where do the terms fit in the scope and sequence for visual grammar?

To increase the range of this research, please contact the author at the address below with any examples of teaching terminology and children's vocabulary use/work samples you are willing to share.
<a.simpson@edfac.usyd.edu.au>

... the arts are places and spaces where one can enrich one's life... When taken seriously, the arts have much to teach educators; they could provide the models needed to create schools that genuinely educate.

(Eisner, 2005:20)

11

Reading to allow spaces to play[1]

> Classroom drama removes us from the world of singular truths and plunges us into multiple realities and multiple visions.
>
> *(Taylor, 1996: 36)*

Robyn Ewing

Today, perhaps more than ever before, children need opportunities to go beneath surface meanings of what they read in order to develop their imaginative capabilities. At the same time, they need to be able to challenge how texts are constructed. While acknowledging that decoding and skills development are an important part of the reading process, this chapter focuses particularly on the potential for drama strategies to enable children to move beyond a text so that they become critically literate.

Initially, critical literacy is defined before moving on to a discussion of drama as critical pedagogy. Evidence gathered from research in three primary classrooms in Sydney during the past twelve months, using a multi-site case study methodology, demonstrates how children's literacy outcomes can be enhanced. Teachers' and students' comments are included alongside examples of children's work, to provide their voices about how drama can promote deep understanding of the multiple perspectives around issues that face us in contemporary Australian society.

[1] An earlier version of this chapter was presented at the *Future Directions in Literacy Conference*, 3–4 March 2005, at the University of Sydney.

Critical literacy

As Rowan (2001, 2005) argues so coherently, children of the 21st century need to be critically literate: they need to have an understanding of *how* texts are constructed and are able to be read (interpreted) from different perspectives, as well as how they function in different cultural contexts to communicate a particular set of beliefs and/or values. Space constraints make a discussion of the many definitions of critical literacy impossible. Most definitions, however, cite the following principles based on the work of Freire, as summarised by Lankshear (1994) but with my emphasis:

- analytic habits of thinking, reading, writing, speaking, viewing that *go beneath surface impressions, traditional myths, mere opinions and clichés*;
- an understanding of the social contexts and consequences of any subject matter;
- the ability to discover *the deep meaning* of an event, text, technique, process, image;
- the ability to apply that meaning to the individual's own context (i.e. move from the generic to the personal); and
- the ability to challenge the assumptions underlying texts.

The increasing tendency to measure literacy achievement through national testing regimes actually works against gathering the kind of evidence that demonstrates the development of students' critical literacy as defined above. Process drama, however, employed as one form of critical pedagogy, has the very strong potential to realise every one of the principles outlined by Lankshear. More than that, it can take us beyond ourselves to dream dreams and to transform who we are or want to be.

Quality literacy through drama as critical pedagogy

The essence of process drama (O'Neill, 1995) is the opportunity for students to *enact* or to take on a role, to walk in someone else's shoes (see, for example, Bolton, 1992; Wagner, 1994; O'Neill, 1995; McMaster, 1998; Hertzberg & Ewing, 1998; Kempe, 2001; O'Mara, 2003; Hertzberg, 2004; and Ewing & Simons, 2004). While the use of enactment in enhancing literacy development is well documented by the authors cited above and by many others, drama as pedagogy is not as widely used in primary classrooms as it should be, given its power to transform learning. Process drama, through its embedded learning activities, enables students to understand meanings conveyed. Its use helps students to develop their thinking, "reconnecting ourselves with events and characters, and with understanding these through our always developing engagement with always changing patterns of cultural order" (Freebody, 2005: 11).

Drama strategies, including readers' theatre, storytelling, depiction, teacher in role, mantle of the expert, puppetry, hotseating, improvisation and thought-tracking (Ewing & Simons, 2004), grounded in authentic contexts but distanced from children's actual experiences, can be used in the classroom to support every aspect of critical literacy development. The imagined and physical contexts of drama worlds allow students to go beyond the superficial or stereotypical to explore the making of meanings in a multisensory medium (Baldwin & Fleming, 2003), providing *spaces* (Williams, 1987) and *places* (Gleeson, 2006) *to play*. Drama starts with the students' already rich imaginations, but it can be a sophisticated tool for building decoding, vocabulary, syntactic, discourse and metacognitive skills and knowledge. In addition, drama strategies encourage the dimensions of quality teaching frameworks that are so much a part of current pedagogy discourse (Education Queensland, 2000; NSW Department of Education and Training, 2003).

The remainder of this chapter contextualises and evidences these assertions through the analysis of the teaching of a unit of work to Stage 2 students in three primary classrooms during 2005.

The research context and the participants

Teachers and students in three Sydney Years 3 and 4 classrooms participated in the current study, which is part of a much larger Quality Teaching Project in each school. Two of these schools (Balgowlah Heights and Curl Curl North) are located in the Northern Beaches district of Sydney, and one (Crown St) in the inner city. The school population in each context is very diverse, and students experience a broad range of socioeconomic contexts. In each case, the researcher had been approached by the principal to work as a mentor alongside the teachers, who were keen to develop students' critical literacy. At Curl Curl, funding was provided by a NSW Department of Education and Training Quality Teaching Project, while Balgowlah Heights was part of the national Boys Lighthouse Project, and so the focus was particularly on improving the engagement of a number of male students in the class. Crown St allocated funding from the school's professional learning budget, but has recently won Australian Government Quality Teaching funding to continue its project.

The twelve teachers involved across the three schools ranged from an early career teacher to one with more than twenty-five years' teaching experience. At the beginning of the project, individual teachers in each school were released to work with the mentor, to identify their concerns or needs in light of the system and school expectations, and strategic goals and directions, and to discuss what unit of work was to be taught in their class. The teachers thus controlled the whole process and self-identified needs in the context of their own classes. Evaluations of more recent professional learning projects across Australia (e.g. the Australian Quality Teaching Projects) have recognised the imperative for teachers to drive their own professional learning (see, for example, Ewing et al., 2004; Ewing et al., 2005).

Each week, over one or two terms, the mentor modelled strategies in the classroom. The class teacher built on these sessions in light of the class needs and her own focus for the particular unit of work. One unit used in all three classes was based on Anthony Hill's *The Burnt Stick.* Chosen because of its rendition of a child, John, stolen from his Aboriginal mother, never to see her again, the story enables children to examine this aspect of Australian history from the multiple perspectives of John himself, his mother, a tribal elder, the Big Man from Welfare, and the station-owner's wife. It provides an example of the authentic literacy texts mentioned in Chapters 4 and 5. As Ann Mason (2005) writes, teachers have a responsibility to share stories that "highlight the inequities and injustices that continue to prevail in our world", but at the same time present them in ways that empower children to "counterbalance the prevailing negativity and helplessness" by focusing on more positive images. Mason (2005: 1) writes:

> Perhaps as we teach and learn ourselves to focus on peace-building in the everyday stories we share rather than the violence, terrorism and racism, this simple beginning may help make this world a happier and more peaceful place for everyone.

A summary of the unit divided into teaching sessions appears below. It must be emphasised that the teachers extended many of the ideas presented briefly here, depending on their students' needs, interests and engagement in the unit. For example, one teacher was particularly keen to develop her students' ability to work cooperatively in small groups. Another was concerned to challenge her male students intellectually, given that their ability was not being realised in the quality of their responses to classroom tasks.

***The Burnt Stick* (Andrew Hill) Integrated Unit**

Developed by Robyn Ewing and Peter Colwell

Suitability:	Years 3–8
Duration:	10 sessions approx 25–40 minutes each over several weeks.
Focus:	*English:* Reading and understanding narrative and factual texts, creating their own factual and fictional texts.
	Human Society and its Environment: Developing an understanding of the issues around the stolen generations and reconciliation.
	Creative Arts: Crayon and charcoal drawing, voice collage, depiction, tapping in and hotseating to explore the concept of 'home' as well as Indigenous/white issues around the stolen generations.

Anticipated outcomes:

It is anticipated that during the unit students will:

- explore a range of factual and fictional texts around the stolen generations;
- examine this controversial period of Australia's history from a range of different perspectives;
- translate textual descriptions to images;
- work cooperatively in small groups to discuss and depict their understandings;
- use their bodies to represent critical moments in a narrative text and convey different moods, thoughts and feelings;
- demonstrate their understanding of different perspectives through a Plus/Minus/Interesting (PMI) chart;
- explore the differences between narrative and exposition;
- write in role as one of the characters in the story;
- write an exposition arguing their point of view clearly; and
- articulate their understanding of 'reconciliation'.

Session 1: Students brainstorm emotion words that describe how they feel about their home (or special place). They choose one word from their list to depict. In a circle, they take turns to say and depict their word. Percussion instruments can be used with the words spoken by the students to create a voice collage. This activity is repeated to represent how they would feel if they were taken from their home and not allowed to return. To the count of ten, students can transform from a feeling of warmth/acceptance/security to one of isolation/despair, etc.

Session 2: In pairs, students read a newspaper article/factual report to build up their field knowledge about the stolen generations. They record their understandings on a mindmap. Teacher leads a discussion about the knowledge that students have developed about this topic.

Session 3: Teacher reads the opening pages of *The Burnt Stick* without showing students the illustrations. Students use oil pastels to sketch their image of the idyllic Pearl Bay Mission. Teacher reads the description of Dryborough Station, and students draw it. A display of the images of Pearl Bay Mission vs. Dryborough Station is built up on the classroom wall, with quotes from the text alongside the children's drawings

Session 4: Students read the rest of the story in small groups and discuss their reactions to John's experiences.

Session 5: In small groups, students choose three critical moments from the story to present as still images/freeze frames. The class views these. The teacher 'taps in' to find out how different characters are feeling. The still images can be recorded with a digital/conventional camera. These are then used for assessment of students' understanding of the issues raised through the text. Students can also write captions to accompany the critical moments chosen.

Session 6: Students choose four or five characters they would like to hotseat (e.g. Mrs Grainger, John, Jabal, the Big Man from Welfare, John's mum, one of John's friends). Allocate one character to each group. In small groups, students then develop questions that are of most interest to them. They can also prioritise these questions. Five students are chosen to be the characters. Students then hotseat them. Later, students choose one of the characters and write in role, describing what happened from this perspective.

Session 7: Teacher introduces a PMI inventory and models some examples. Students then complete their own PMI chart about the practice of removing Indigenous students from their families.

Session 8: Teacher models the structure of an exposition using the issues around the stolen generations as a topic. Students contribute their ideas using their inventories. A number of subsequent writing sessions can follow in which students take a current issue in their local community and develop their own exposition. Later, these are shared in small groups and discussed.

Session 9: Older groups can watch *Rabbit Proof Fence* and discuss how the issues are presented through the medium of film contrasted with the written text.

Session 10: Students brainstorm words that encapsulate the concept of reconciliation using the understandings they have developed over the last ten sessions. Which words are most meaningful for them? If desired, these words can be depicted as for Session 1. Students choose five words of most relevance for them and write them on hand-cutouts that have been decorated.

Additional related sessions: Students can spend time immersing themselves in Indigenous art and stories, depending on time and the purposes of the unit.

N.B. Further details about the drama strategies can be found in Ewing and Simons (2004).

Findings

A range of methods was used to collect data in order to evaluate the process together with the learning outcomes. Examples of students' work were collected, with permission from both students and parents. Students reflected on the unit at its conclusion. Each teacher was engaged in conversational interviews about the process, both with the researcher and more formally with their principal. In two schools, an independent evaluator was employed to conduct interviews with the teachers. In one school, he also undertook focus group discussions with groups of students. The evaluator (Loughland, 2005a: 7) writes in one report:

> High expectations of the students were also apparent in the Year 4 classroom where ____ was mentoring an early career teacher in literacy pedagogy. The students were able to describe to me how the activities led them to a deep understanding of the themes of two texts, *Boy Overboard* and *The Burnt Stick*. [...] The conversation I had with these four students revealed their deep understanding of characters, themes and meaning of texts. This finding was supported by the teacher, who has noticed that the students engage with texts at a deeper level since these activities and strategies were introduced at the beginning of the year.

A selection of student comments and excerpts from their writing and drawing appear on the following pages:

On the value of drama:

- *Drama was good because we got to feel how John Jagamarra felt.*
- *I think it was a great way of learning what happened with Aboriginals and why it happened.*
- *I liked writing what it was like at Pearl Bay Mission that put your mind to the text and you had to think what is was like back then.*

In writing about the critical incidents chosen, one student commented that he chose: *... when the big man from welfare is standing over me ready to take me away. When I woke I saw him standing on top of me. I was feeling very angry and scared because I didn't know what he will do to me.*

Another, choosing Liyan, John's mother, wrote: *John's mother is sad because they would take her beloved son away.*

Writing in role as John, another student wrote: *I miss my mum and my family. I wish I was back at Dryborough with my family. I wish I could swim in the pool in the creek where we used to swim after rain and lie on the lizard rock where we would lie afterwards sunning ourselves after our swim.*

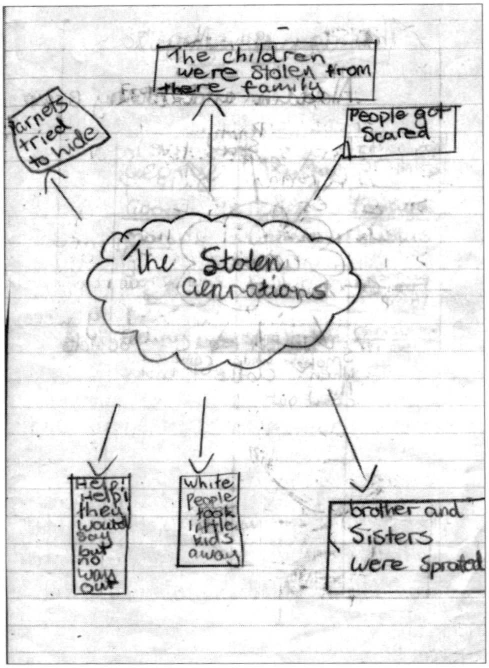

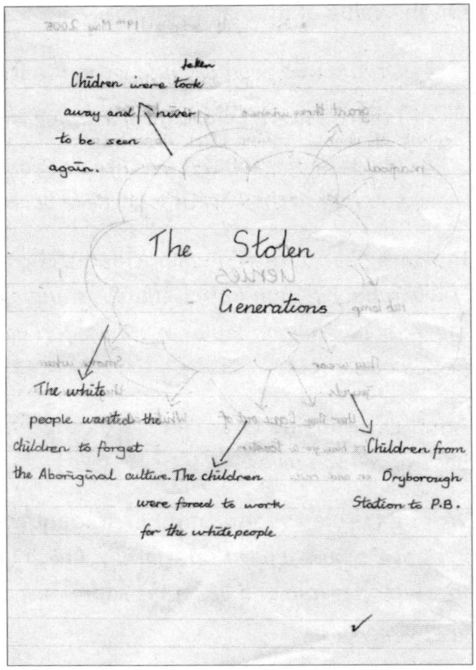

In each context, the unit stimulated the students' understanding of a complex issue from a range of different perspectives. Each of the teachers commented that their students' oracy, reading and writing skills had improved markedly over the term. This chapter is not arguing that this unit of work was the sole reason for this improvement in student literacy outcomes. At the same time, however, the teachers and students felt strongly that the use of drama with authentic texts had been an important factor in this improvement. At Balgowlah Heights, where boys' engagement was the focus, the teacher cited a range of examples where the boys in her class had worked hard on the activities in the unit, producing high-quality responses to the issues raised. She particularly noted the power of hotseating and depiction as strategies that were successful in engaging these students. One boy in the class was accepted into group activities for the first time and, also for the first time, was able to work cooperatively. In addition, teachers commented on the improvement in students' overall ability to work cooperatively. Many of these outcomes and the understandings that the students developed cannot easily be measured in the kinds of test situations that currently dominate our assessment practices. Yet this type of evidence is important.

Conclusion

Australian politicians and educational policymakers must move beyond preoccupations with the measurement of technical literacy outcomes. Such evidence is only one side of the story. Drama provides important opportunities for all students to read to develop their imaginations, to see beyond surface or stereotypical meanings and to develop their own use of language. Children can produce interesting and sensitive written and oral work as a result of working collaboratively on sculpting and depiction in pairs and small groups. Tapping in enables them to play with words and give particular attention to what words they will choose to communicate their emotions. Looking at each other's depictions also helps them honour each other's work and, at the same time, realise that there are many alternative meanings and interpretations of a text.

In the above unit, students were able to understand that there are always multiple perspectives about historical events and often no one 'right' answer. The students moved from talking and drawing to reading and writing – from an expressive use of oral language to a more abstract use of language.

The use of drama in primary classrooms can facilitate the development of student imaginations, build on their creativity and, at the same time, improve their literacy skills. If students develop their own understandings of who they are through walking in others' shoes, they will in time hopefully transform their world and see new possibilities. This chapter demonstrates clearly how important it is to bring drama strategies together with authentic literature to encourage primary students to read beyond the text, to walk in someone else's shoes, and so develop critical literacy.

References

Baldwin, P., & Fleming, K. (2003) *Teaching literacy through drama*. London: Routledge Falmer.

Bolton, G. (1992) *New perspectives on classroom drama*. London: Simon and Schuster.

Department of Education, Science and Training (DEST) (2005). *Teaching Reading: Report and Recommendations*. Canberra: Commonwealth of Australia.

Education Queensland (2000) *New Basics Project*. Brisbane: Department of Education.

Eisner, E. (2005) 'Opening a shuttered wisdom: An introduction to a Special Section on the arts and the intellect'. *Phi Delta Kappan*, September, 87(1).

Eisner, E. (2005) Teaching for artistic behaviour. Keynote address, National Arts Education Conference, Boston.

Ewing, R., & Simons, J. (2004) *Beyond the script Take 2: Drama in the classroom*. Sydney: Primary English Teaching Association.

Ewing, R., Smith, D., Anderson, M., Gibson, R., & Manuel, J. (2004) *Teachers as learners*. Evaluation of Australian Government Quality Teaching Program/NSW Department of Education and Training Quality Teaching, Action Learning. Sydney: NSW Department of Education and Training.

Ewing, R., Hoban, G., Hetherington, T., Anderson, J., Smith, D., & Kervin, L. (2005) *Evaluative inquiry into the sustainability of teacher professional learning through action learning*. Sydney: NSW Department of Education and Training.

Gleeson, L. (2006). 'Places to play. Stories as an adventure playground'. Paper presented at the Future Directions in Literacy Conference, University of Sydney, March, 2006.

Hertzberg, M. (2004) 'Unpacking the drama process as intellectually rigorous – The teacher gives you the bones of it and we have to act the muscles'. *Drama Australia Journal*, 28(2): 41–53.

Hertzberg, M., & Ewing, R. (1998) 'Developing our imagination: Enactment and critical literacy'. *Primary English Teaching Note 116*. Sydney: Primary English Teaching Association.

Kempe, A. (2001) 'Drama as a framework for the development of literacy'. *Set 2*, 14–19.

Lankshear, C. (1994) *Critical literacy*. Occasional Paper No. 3. Belconnen, Canberra: Australian Curriculum Studies Association.

Loughland, A. (2005). *Professional learning evaluation*. Unpublished reports, Curl Curl North and Crown St Primary Schools.

Mason, A. (2005) *For the sake of the children. Peace-building storytelling activities for teachers, parents and adults who work with children*. Teaching and Learning for Peace Foundation. Accessed 30/3/2006 at: <http://www.tlpeace.org.au/>

McMaster, J. (1998) 'Doing literature: Using drama to build literacy'. *The Reading Teacher*, 51(7): 574–584.

NSW Department of Education and Training (2003) *Quality teaching in NSW government schools: A discussion paper.* Sydney: NSW Department of Education and Training, Professional Support and Curriculum Directorate.

O'Mara, J. (2003) 'Repositioning drama to centre stage: Drama, English, text and literacy'. *Drama Australia Journal*, 27(2): 17–26.

O'Neill, C. (1995) *Dramaworlds: A framework for process drama*. London: Heinemann.

Rowan, L. (2001) *Write me in: Inclusive texts in the primary classroom*. Sydney: Primary English Teaching Association.

Rowan, L. (2005) 'Journeying towards literacy: Are we there yet?' *Occasional Paper No. 1*. Sydney: Primary English Teaching Association.

Taylor, P. (1996) *Researching drama and arts education: Paradigms and possibilities*. New York: Falmer.

Wagner, B. (1994) 'The effects of role playing on persuasive letters of fourth and eighth graders'. *English in Australia*, 108: 29–37.

Williams, G. (1987) 'Space to play: The analysis of narrative structure in classroom work with children's literature. In M. Saxby and G. Winch (Eds.), *Give them wings: The experience of children's literature*. Melbourne: Macmillan.

Acknowledgements

Thanks to the principals, teachers and students at Crown St, Curl Curl North and Balgowlah Heights primary schools who so willingly shared their classrooms, responses and work samples.

Afterword
Going forward together

Robyn Ewing

Australian teachers are certainly experiencing conditions of anxiety and pressure in a country whose current government has politicised education generally and the teaching of reading specifically more than ever before. Yet it is clear that quality teachers certainly make a difference to the lives and learning outcomes of the children they teach, and we must focus on this.

As this book was being readied for publication, another study confirming the important role that teachers play in children's literacy development, *In teachers' hands* (Louden et al., 2005), was receiving some media attention across Australia. This study focused on the differences between effective and less effective literacy teachers of children in their first two years of school. The research team included some of the committee members from the National Inquiry into the Teaching of Literacy. In each state, 2000 children were assessed at the start and end of the year. Researchers then visited schools in Victoria, NSW, Queensland and Tasmania to observe children and teachers working in classrooms. While all the teachers used the same kinds of literacy activities (e.g. shared book reading, phonics, modelled writing), the most effective teachers, whose students made the biggest gains in literacy over the year, drew on a much wider repertoire of teaching practices. These teachers demonstrated deeper knowledge of their subject and were able to diagnose the individual needs of their students and plan accordingly. In doing so, they were able to challenge their students intellectually while ensuring that learning was fun. It's interesting to note that while all teachers programmed study of letter–sound relationships, those who were less effective tended to teach phonics in isolation rather than within meaningful contexts. They relied more on busywork than on engaging tasks.

It is thus imperative that we focus on ensuring that teachers have constant opportunities to extend and update their professional knowledge about how they can meet the needs of diverse groups of learners as they learn to become literate in a multiplicity of ways. As a community, we need to recognise and celebrate teachers as the experts they are.

Let's move beyond the reading wars and stop separating out various components of the learning-to-read process and fighting over which part is more important at which point. Different children will need different approaches and strategies at different points in their learning journey. Identifying and using all knowledge about processes of learning to read, along with an extensive range of strategies and excellent resources, is vital. The centrality of the use of real children's literature and other authentic factual, multimedia and community texts, along with conversations about how these relate to our own lives, cannot be overstated. As Margaret Meek has said, it is the texts themselves that do a great deal of the teaching. We must therefore ensure that we find the spaces and places for our children to develop a love of reading and an understanding of how much it can enrich their lives.

References

Louden, W., Rohl, M, Barratt-Pugh, C., Brown, C., Cairney, T., Elderfield, J., House, H., Meiers, M., Rivalland, J., & Rowe, K. (2005) *In teachers' hands: Effective literacy teaching practices in the early years of schooling*. Canberra, ACT: Australian Government Department of Education, Science and Training.

Meek, M. (1988) *How texts teach what readers learn*. Stroud, UK: Thimble Press.

Nichols, S. (2003) Reading the social world. In H. Comber & J. Barnett (Eds), *Look again*. Sydney: Primary English Teaching Association.